Andr ri
Giuli

ıre
ɛpolo
ɪangone
_a Molinari

ON THE ROAD city
Naples

ON THE ROAD
Editor of collection
Laura Andreini

editorial project
Forma Edizioni srl, Firenze, Italia
redazione@formaedizioni.it
www.formaedizioni.it

editorial direction
Laura Andreini

authors
Andrea Nastri
Giuliana Vespere

editorial staff
Maria Giulia Caliri
Livia D'Aliasi
Andrea Benelli

graphic design
Isabella Peruzzi
Alessandra Smiderle

translations
Katy Hannan
Karen Tomatis

photolithography
LAB di Gallotti Giuseppe Fulvio, Florence

texts by
Laura Andreini
Pasquale Belfiore
Bruno Discepolo
Fabio Mangone
Luca Molinari

Andrea Nastri, Architect, PhD in History of Architecture, is Adjunct Professor at LUM Jean Monnet University and specialises in monumental restoration and urban requalification for the Municipality of Naples. His articles are published in newspapers and international specialized periodicals and he is the author of several books on architecture.

Giuliana Vespere, Architect, PhD in Architectural and Urban Design, is Adjunct Professor at LUM Jean Monnet University and is an official of the Municipality of Naples. She is the author of several essays and has curated a number of publications on modern and contemporary architecture. She is a member of the Board of Directors of Fondazione dell'Ordine Architetti PPC of Naples and its Province.

First Edition: February 2019

ISBN 978-88-99534-68-4

Images and drawings on pages 36-37, 42, 52, 84, 86-87, 94, 104, 110, 112, 122, 126, 128, 170, 174, 186, 196, 198 were taken from Sergio Stenti, Vito Cappiello (edited by), *NapoliGuida e dintorni: itinerari di architettura moderna*, CLEAN Edizioni, Naples, 2010 by curtesy of the publisher.

Table of contents

Guidebook as tool

On the Road is a collection of contemporary architecture guidebooks whose purpose is to tell about a place, whether a city or larger area, through its architectural works chosen to be visited and experienced directly.

The guidebook has a convenient special jacket that opens into a map marking the location of the architectural works and interesting sites to visit. On the back are miniature images and addresses of the architectural works described in detail within.

The book starts with short essays explaining the city or area's present day and history and outlining possible future scenarios with planned or imminent projects. Each work features a photograph of the whole, an architectural drawing (plan or section), a short description, and facts including architect, type, year of construction, address, website, and how to visit it.

The finest architecture of each city and suggested routes are represented by this collection of not-to-be-missed, "timeless" buildings that uniquely define their settings. General information and useful tips for travelers help them optimize their visits and quickly understand the essence of the place described.

Museums, theatres, restaurants, hotels and a list of top architectural firms working in the city let visitors turn a regular trip into an opportunity for study or work.

Note: The pinpoints outside the maps at the beginning of the itineraries are viewable on the rear of the book jacket.

Naples

Laura Andreini*

Each book in the On the Road series tells the story of a city through its most important works of contemporary architecture. For some cities, more than others, the narrative is more complex and labyrinthine; there is a fine line between contemporary and modern architecture, and moreover, historic architecture does not simply exist as a backdrop set behind new interventions, but is an integral part of a narrative inside which the actual incorporation of all aspects plays a major role. Therefore it is difficult to illustrate certain areas without making reference to this fusion, and describing the continuing sequence of ancient, modern and contemporary architecture.

Naples is one of these cities: a very ancient metropolitan territory; centuries of urban fabric layers, as many as the number of its dominating rulers; a territorial expansion that has resiliently adapted to the undulating configuration of the landscape, while managing to achieve a strictly orthogonal "forma urbis", as in the ancient city centre.

The invitation we extend to those who wish to visit contemporary Naples is to walk its streets identifying the architectural works that belong to the modern school, with a view to understanding the intention, criteria, and approach of the designers of the most recent architectural interventions. There is a common thread in the composition and method.

An interesting aspect is the fact that the most recent works created in Naples are part of the wider infrastructural projects for the city, with the new Metro railway system and its iconic Metro stations. This project began at the beginning of the new millennium and is still creating transformations in urban mobility and public spaces, in those areas where the stations are not limited to underground spaces, but often emerge above ground. In a city that is somewhat hostile to high calibre contemporary interventions, excellence has chosen to descend into subterranean passages, symbolic of a city often defined as "contradictory" for the alternating aspects of beauty and degradation, chaos and tranquillity, lethargy and innovation.

The guide to Naples proposes five itineraries that lead from the historic city centre, first in a Westward direction, then towards the Northern outskirts, finally moving Eastwards not far from Vesuvius. These itineraries do not only take the visitor from one place to another, but also along a passage through history, moving from the Castel dell'Ovo, the initial monument in this guide, to the Cinema teatro Augusteo by Foschini and Nervi as far as the newly constructed "Municipio" Metro station, designed by Siza and Souto de Moura. This itinerary that meanders through centuries of history, is a privilege that Naples is able to offer its visitors.

* Laura Andreini is Architect and Associate Professor at DIDA, University of Florence. Co-founder of Studio Archea where she still works, she is also writer and Deputy Editor for *area* magazine.

Political / geographical facts

country
Italy

language
italian

area code
+39 081

coordinates
40°50 N
14°15 E

area
117.27 sq. km

population
962,260

density
8,205.51 inhabitants / sq. km

time zone
UTC+1

city website
www.comune.napoli.it

Administrative districts

1. Chiaia, Posillipo, San Ferdinando
2. Avvocata, Montecalvario, Pendino,
   Porto, Mercato, San Giuseppe
3. Stella, San Carlo all'Arena
4. San Lorenzo, Vicaria, Poggioreale,
   Zona Industriale
5. Vomero, Arenella
6. Ponticelli, Barra,
   San Giovanni a Teduccio
7. Miano, Secondigliano,
   San Pietro a Patierno
8. Piscinola, Marianella,
   Scampia, Chiaiano
9. Soccavo, Pianura
10. Bagnoli, Fuorigrotta

General information
useful addresses and numbers

INFORMATION OFFICES

Azienda autonoma di soggiorno, cura e turismo Piazza del Gesù
Piazza del Gesù Nuovo 28
+39 081 5512701
Mon - Sun / 9 am - 1 pm

Ufficio informazioni EPT Capodichino
Capodichino International Airport,
Viale F. Ruffo di Calabria
+39 081 7896734
Mon - Sun / 9 am - 8 pm

Ufficio Informazioni EPT Stazione Centrale
Piazza Garibaldi
+39 081 268779
Mon - Sun / 9 am - 7.30 pm

EMERGENCY SERVICES

Carabinieri 112
Police 113
Polizia Stradale 081 5954111/081 2208311
Fire Department 115
Guardia di Finanza 117
Polizia Municipale 081 7513177
Guardia costiera 1530

URBAN TRANSPORT*

ANM
(buses, alibuses, trams, Line 1 subway and funicular lines) www.anm.it
Trenitalia
(line 2 subway) www.trenitalia.com
Circumvesuviana, Cumana, Circumflegrea
www.eavsrl.it
Unico Campania
www.unicocampania.it
CTP
www.ctp.na.it
Subway
Subway Line 1 (ANM) the Art Metro – connecting the central station with the more elevated areas of the city reaching the northern area of Piscinola. In the future, this line will reach Capodichino Airport.
Subway Line 2 (Trenitalia) connecting the central station to Pozzuoli.
Subway Line 6 (ANM) the latest line with four stations on the Fuorigrotta-Mergellina route. In the future this line will be extended to Piazza del Municipio via the Chiaia neighbourhood, intersecting with Line 1.
Funicular Lines (ANM) four lines: Centrale, Chiaia, and Montesanto serve the Vomero neighbourhood; the Mergellina funicular line connects Posillipo to Mergellina.
Cumana and Circumflegrea (EAV) historical railway lines connecting the centre of Naples (Montesanto) with the western part of the city and the towns of Pozzuoli, Bacoli and Quarto.
Circumvesuviana (EAV) railway line connecting Naples-Corso Garibaldi to the southern and eastern areas of the city all the way to Salerno and Avellino, reaching the densely populated towns of the Sorrento peninsula and Pompeii.

Taxi
+39 081 8888; +39 081 0101; +39 081 5707070

GENERAL CONSULATE OF THE UNITED STATES
Piazza della Repubblica 2, 80122
+39 081 5838111

GENERAL CONSULATE OF GREAT BRITAIN
Via dei Mille 40, 80121
+39 081 4238379

GENERAL CONSULATE OF FRANCE
Via Crispi 86, 80121
+39 081 5980711

GENERAL CONSULATE OF RUSSIA
Via Partenope 1, 80121
+39 081 19205031

HOW TO PHONE

From a local landline: dial local code number followed by phone number (081)

From a foreign landline: dial international code (+39) city code (081) and phone number

* Subway Lines 1 and 6, buses and funicular lines are run by ANM Azienda Napoletana Mobilità s.p.a.
Subway Line 2 is run by Trenitalia.
Line and service interchange is facilitated by an integrated fare policy and by assuring travel continuity at interchange stations.

Useful tips

1. When visiting Naples, it is generally better to travel by rail rather than by road, as vehicles are often subject to long traffic jams. The four **funicular railways** are comfortable and reliable (three connect the Vomero area to the city centre, and the other links Posillipo with Mergellina). The **Metro** system is worth a special mention. The Linea 1 connects the northern outskirts and the central station passing through Vomero and the historic city centre, and is the line of the renowned Naples Art Metro Stations designed by distinguished international architects with a lot of contemporary art works, but the delays are a little long for a metro service. Linea 2 is a metropolitan railway system managed by Trenitalia, connecting the eastern outskirts with Pozzuoli, crossing the whole city in the east-west direction, with frequent trains running every 8-10 minutes.

2. Naples is a city with outstanding museums, especially the MANN, one of the world's most important archaeological museums; the **Museum of Capodimonte/69** that houses the precious Farnese collection, the Museo Nazionale di San Martino, located in the Charter house by the same name, the Museo del Tesoro di San Gennaro in the **Duomo/20**, and naturally the famous **Madre Museum/21**. The **Campania Artecard** (www.campaniartecard.it) is a pass that provides discounts and advantages for access to art and culture centres in Naples and the Campania region with cheaper rates on public transport.

3. One of the best ways to discover the city is **on foot**, wandering through the narrow streets of the ancient city centre, or strolling through the large city parks; the views are worth the climb up the picturesque steep stairway streets to the Neapolitan hills from the city centre and the sea: the most popular are the Pedamentina di San Martino, the Gradini del Petraio, and the Calata San Francesco. Beautiful **parks** include the Virgiliano on the Posillipo Hill, and not far away, the Pausilypon archaeological park with the submerged Gaiola marine area where visitors can view the remains of ancient villas, moorings, and statues of nymphs and the ancient Roman tunnel of Seiano that traverses the whole Posillipo tuff stone mountain through to the Phlegraean peninsula. Other beautiful green spaces are the Real Bosco di Capodimonte, the Villa Floridiana Park, and the **Villa Comunale/25**.

4. Another fascinating aspect of the city can be seen in the **"hidden" Naples**, that conceals amazing traces of its many historical layers in the underground caves and tunnels carved into the tuff stone. Especially interesting is "underground" Naples: a series of grottos and tunnels where the tuff stone was quarried for the construction of the city since its very origins. Later the Romans developed a network of tunnels and water cisterns to distribute the water from the Serino spring; the archaeological remains of Macellum, the ancient Roman market, can be seen beneath the Basilica of San Lorenzo; the Bourbon tunnel, the secret underground passage between the Palazzo Reale and Piazza Vittoria, was built in 1855 to give King Ferdinand II a rapid escape route in the case of danger. It was later converted into a shelter during World War 2, and finally used to store municipal judicial archives. Naples is also known for its **arcane aspects**, the most famous being the Fontanelle Cemetery in the Sanità district; a former quarry, it was converted into a burial ground during the plague that struck the city in 1654.

5. Naples is a city built on hills and is famous for its great **observation points** with unparalleled views of the Bay of Naples. One of the most popular can be seen from Piazzale di San Martino on the peak of the Vomero Hill; the panorama from the parade ground of Castel Sant'Elmo is even wider, with 180 degree views from east to west. More wonderful views can be seen from the Villa Floridiana gardens not very far away. Higher up, is the Eremo dei Camaldoli, whose belvedere provides the widest reaching panorama of the whole Bay. Famous, and extremely popular, is the belvedere of Sant'Antonio at Posillipo, rising steeply from Mergellina. A vast panorama of the city can be seen from Parco Virgiliano, on the Posillipo Hill, with views of the south-east side of the Bay of Naples and the island of Capri on the horizon, west of the former industrial area of Bagnoli, and overlooking the Phlegraean Fields.

6. A worthwhile experience for those visiting Naples in summer is to **go for a swim in the city**, at Marechiaro, at Gaiola, at the Baia delle rocce verdi, along the Trentaremi coast with its underwater rocks, or at the well-known Lido beaches at Posillipo, like the historic Bagno Elena, fascinating for its legendary Villa Donn'Anna, that seems to rise straight from the sea. The city council has promoted a range of activities during the summer to make the bay more accessible to tourists and the local population, with walking routes along the coast, and kayak trips to view the beautiful villas that overlook the Bay.

7. Naples offers a vast range of inexpensive gastronomical delights including street food, pastry cafés, and trattoria restaurants. Naturally, Naples is famous as the home of the pizza and the "traditional art of Neapolitan pizza making", which was recently included in the UNESCO Intangible Cultural Heritage list. When strolling through the old city centre there are certain obligatory **gastronomical halts**: folded over **pizza**, Pasta omelette and crocchè are quintessential Neapolitan street food. The most famous **cakes** include babà, pastiera and sfogliatelle to be enjoyed in one of the legendary pastry cafés. And for those who want a gift, stop at the Gay-Odin Chocolaterie, with its delicious bonbons in beautifully decorated boxes with Neapolitan gouache scenes.

A guide for reading, visiting and evaluating the city

Pasquale Belfiore*

This guide is designed for the contemporary traveller who is not in a hurry, since haste is one of the most obvious aspects of stressful modern tourism. This book contains written pages that demand an instant to pause and absorb each monument, building, landscape or aspect that deserves a moment of appreciation; like all Art Cities. Like Naples, that today offers visitors a view of each of the "new cities" that have succeeded one another throughout history confirming the root origin: *nea-polis*, a city within another, laid on top of another, alongside another, never completely eradicating the previous urban history. Like all the guides in this series, the architectural stratification described in this book begins with the contemporary, and travels backward in time, selecting architectural paradigms of the close and distant past without which our concept of today appears fragmented and incomprehensible. An exemplary choice, especially in the city of Benedetto Croce, who said: "All history is contemporary history".

So, the young editors, Andrea Nastri and Giuliana Vespere, focussed on Naples and its architecture of excellence, interweaving examples chosen for their architectural value and notoriety with unexpected and audacious tour proposals, so that visitors could discover once more the *beautiful*, the *ancient*, and the *unconventional* aspects of Naples described in the 17th century guide by Carlo Celano. In this way, the nucleus of powerful structures of the past (Castel dell'Ovo, Castel Nuovo, Castel Capuano, Palazzo Reale and Reggia di Capodimonte, Albergo dei Poveri, Certosa di San Martino) sits in contrast with Liberty style villas and apartment buildings and their discrete decorative elegance. This style is followed by the architecture of the Fascist Regime, exemplified in the Exhibition of Italian Overseas Territories (1940) and the Rione Carità, with its Post Office Building (one of the masterpieces of 20th century Italian architecture) and the great post war constructions like the Central station, the football stadium, Politecnico university, Policlinico hospital complex, and more recently, the Città della Scienza at Bagnoli. Lastly, the controversial Administrative Centre coexists with the Metropolitan Art Stations designed by famous international architects, an unusual but impressive fusion of architecture and figurative art. Crossing over the municipal boundaries, it is possible to visit architecture of excellence like the Olivetti Factory at Pozzuoli designed by Luigi Cosenza, or the High Speed Railway Station at Afragola, by Zaha Hadid.

This guide fully confirms the opinions often expressed on this city: exceptional for its past architecture and urban planning; but following the later half of the 20th century, with relatively few outstanding buildings, described correctly in this guide. The future of contemporary Naples remains a problem.

* Pasquale Belfiore, Tenured Professor in Architectural Design at the Luigi Vanvitelli University, has written books and articles on contemporary architectural history and analysis. He was a Municipal Councillor for the historic centre of the city of Naples.

Naples, the dual city

Bruno Discepolo*

Aristocratic and well-cultured, but proletarian and plebeian at the same time, Naples is a contradictory, dual-sided city. For centuries, it has represented the archetype of the Mediterranean city, admitting that such a category exists and is able to unify the urban models of countries on both sides of the Mediterranean sea. Inscribed in its genetics, form, and settlement – from ancient Palepolis, along the line which goes from Megaride-Monte Echia to the new city of Neapolis – more than any other, Parthenope embodies the epitome of the archaic Mediterranean coastal city, as described by Fernard Braudel.

Since its foundation, Naples has continued to grow, to expand, as if part of an uninterrupted discourse, but whose lexicon has changed over time. For most of its 2500 years of history, the city has continued to take shape, creating routes for the development and anthropization of its landscape modelled on the conformation of the coastline, following the curves of the bay, climbing the slopes and hills (San Martino, Posillipo, Miradois, Camaldoli, Capodimonte) descending again into the valleys as far as the beaches of Chiaia, or moving further east along the course of the Sebeto river. But at the same time, Naples defined its "forma urbis" within specific urban guidelines, with blueprints that are recognisable still today in the ancient city centre and the three *plateiai* (modern decumani) represented by the roads of San Biagio, Tribunali and Anticaglia. Here too, in the foundations of Neapolis, we can trace the origins of a dialogue that has never been interrupted, between deference to nature and conformation with place, and the aspiration for rule and order within a rational formal project: a dialogue maybe nowhere else so recognizable in a city of ancient foundation. In fact, in the original plains facing the sea, recent research has discovered traces of a geometrical layout, and the division of the space by a circle and a square based on the Golden Ratio ("sectioning a line in extreme and mean ratio"). This leads us to suppose that Naples was in fact the reference model for the "Ideal City" of Vitruvius.

But rationality and geometry were also the foundations for successive urban planning schemes like the layout for the Quartieri Spagnoli, above Via Toledo, or the redevelopment plan following the cholera epidemic in 1884, with the construction of the long straight boulevard (Corso Umberto I) inspired by Haussman, and many other quarters in the centre and outskirts of the city, including Fuorigrotta, Vomero, Vasto, and the *rioni* of Carità, Materdei, and Arenaccia.

Successively, especially after the Second World War and later, there was a frenzy of construction that tended to saturate every inch of terrain that was still free, mostly for speculation and almost always lacking in any form of architectural quality. The previous difficult balance between organicistic trends and respect for the *genius loci* and rationalistic, or even simply academic or formal planning schemes, collapsed in the name of spontaneous, haphazard, and frequently, illegal constructions, especially in the city centre, symmetrical to the contemporary urban sprawl in the vast metropolitan area.

For decades, at least since the 1970s, the technical and political debate in Naples (but also the previsions of the General Urban Planning Scheme itself, drawn up in 1972) focussed on a way to move large numbers of the population away from the ancient city centre. Paradoxically, the urban plan did not produce concrete effects on the program for the physical transformation of the city, which did however lose a fifth of its population between the early 1980s and the first decade of the new millennium. The population dropped to less than a million inhabitants at a time when, in other areas, urban densification policies were being developed.

Less focus was placed on the possibility of modernising Naples on a par with other European and Italian cities – as occurred in Milan and Turin – through urban renewal projects for entire districts, and including the incorporation of quality architecture. This explains, at least in part, why there is such a scarcity of contemporary architecture in a city which was a cultural hub and the capital of a realm, with a direct influence over a widespread metropolitan area, and even over the whole southern region of Italy. It may also be the reason why it is necessary to return to the Modernist period to retrace the most important interventions in recent Neapolitan history, both in terms of urban transformation (the expansion of the city towards the west, the opening up of Viale Augusto and the creation of the Mostra d'Oltremare) as well as of individual examples of architecture (the Post Office Building by Giuseppe Vaccaro).

Nor is it coincidental that among the more recent interventions in the city, the large majority belong to a project to update infrastructures, with the construction of the new subway system. This monumental project, which has been under way for decades, has not only provided the city and the wider metropolitan area with a modern transport system, but through the excavation work, has succeeded in making important discoveries about a large part of the city's history uncovering considerable material evidence (the port and the ships found at Piazza Municipio, the Gymnasium, and the ancient temple in Piazza Nicola Amore). This has led to the creation of the Art and Archaeology Subway Stations, designed by important architects (Siza, Souto de Moura, Perrault, Tusquets, Podrecca, Aulenti). While, in the majority of cases, the project has produced underground architecture, in others, with great impact, the interventions have emerged above ground (Mendini's Salvator Rosa and Materdei stations) invading streets and squares in a felicitous fusion of artistic and environmental redevelopment.

As stated in the introduction, it is difficult to encapsulate the complex and often contradictory nature of Naples in a representational definition. In the same way, strolling around its chaotic crowded streets, twisting lanes, ramps and depots, it would be hard to realise its original aspirations to models of geometrical and urban perfection. But Naples is a combination of all these aspects: order and chaos, beauty and neglect, an obsessive attachment to its own history and identity, together with daring experimentation; and with its vitality, the constantly tangible presence of its population, and its prodigious historical city centre, Naples conserves its principal characteristic as a modern European and Mediterranean city.

* Bruno Discepolo, Architect, taught urban planning courses at the Luigi Vanvitelli University. Previously President of Sirena, the association for the promotion of restoration interventions in the historic centre of Naples, he is currently the Councillor for the Territorial Administration Plan for the Campania Region.

Controversial Modernity

Fabio Mangone*

Even more than in other Italian cities, the situation of "modern construction" in Naples reveals obvious contradictions: compared with the huge mass of drab buildings, aggressive speculation projects and abusive buildings that disfigures the landscape, there are not many examples of excellent architecture with either an aesthetic or social focus, as can be seen among those included in this guide. More than in other cities, there is a huge gap between the quality of average urban buildings and individual examples of high calibre. Already in the late 19th century, during the vast redevelopment and expansion project, more enlightened critics complained about this gap, comparing rare examples of "artistic" architecture, like the Galleria Umberto I, with the large number of mediocre constructions. The situation became more critical in the 20th century, as the concept of "Urban Decorum" decreased. After the decorative period of Liberty, Art Deco, and Neo-eclectic architecture, which produced commendable results, it became increasingly more uncommon for the private sector to promote works of superior aesthetic quality, leaving the prerogative to public intervention. We only need to compare the old rione Carità from the Fascist period, mainly composed of public construction and flanked by institutional buildings, like the Post Office building (a true masterpiece by Giuseppe Vaccaro), with the new post-war rione Carità, scattered with drab, excessively high apartment towers. There is the same divergence in the Fuorigrotta district, between the area centred around the Mostra d'Oltremare, with good quality urban design, and the surrounding residential constructions. After the Second World War, (naturally with certain exceptions) it was usually easier to find better levels of architectural design in subsidised social housing than in private construction. However, often structural elegance and architectural design can be enjoyed more in old photos than in the concrete reality of today. The deterioration suffered by what had formerly been exemplary areas of public building schemes bears witness to the characteristics of a region where abusive construction reigns supreme, but there is also some difficulty among more committed architects to interpret the true needs of the end users. A flagrant example of this lack of understanding is the striking, but notorious "Sails of Scampia"; some consider it the maximum meeting point between local architectural style and international utopistic experimental design, but others, on the contrary, see it as a symbol of degradation. It's another paradox of these architectural artefacts: they seem transplanted from the plan of Tokyo Bay to the "non-place" of Scampia, and therefore, precisely because of their de-contextualised nature, they have become the emblematic symbols of the area.

Because of the considerable gap between good quality buildings and average constructions, "modern architecture" in Naples creates a complicated geographical situation. Sometimes outstanding elements lead to substantial architectural concentration, like the Liberty neighbourhood in Via dei Mille – Parco Margherita, the Rione Carità, the Mostra d'Oltremare, and the Naples Administration District, for example. However, more often, impressive architectural examples simply remain important exercises in style within contexts of total mediocrity, if not degradation. Despite this aspect they are able to provide an important element of direction: this occurred with the Piazza Grande residential complex, the Theology Faculty, the San Giovanni University Centre, not to mention the High Velocity Railway Station. In fact, it is perhaps the architectural design of railway stations and connection infrastructures that provide one of the most defining aspects of modern architecture. Naples was a trail blazer with the first railway in Italy, the Naples-Portici line, built in the 1830s, when it became clear that travelling by mechanical means was an important aspect of modernity. Fifty years later, Lamont Young devised his pioneering plan for a metropolitan railway system: despite the technical validity of the scheme, it was not accepted, like the daring elevated railway on pylons designed by Adolfo Avena. However, during the same period, the innovative Chiaia and Montesanto funicular railways to Vomero were more successful. Since that time, stations have become not only flow management structures, but also cornerstones of modern design. We could quote many examples, but in particular, worth mentioning are the Cumana station designed by Frediano Frediani, "Fuorigrotta" and "Mostra" (the latter, re-designed by Pagliara), the fine Central Station (combined team work by Vaccaro, Zevi and Piccinato), today disfigured by excessive commercial retail additions. There is also the Circumvesuviana terminus, the Afragola High Velocity Railway Station, and above all, the new subway lines: some stations are finished, and others are awaiting completion or construction. This type of infrastructure, considered as state of the art, with attentive research into aesthetic quality in the context of daily life, creates a network of modernity, connecting resilient areas in a city that has the largest historic centre in Europe, if not in the world.

* Fabio Mangone is an Architect, a PhD in History of Architecture, and Tenured Professor of History of Architecture at the Federico II University of Naples. His many ambits of research include the city of Naples and its transformations over the modern and contemporary age.

Neapolitan Archipelago

Luca Molinari*

Naples is not a conventional city, but still one of those few places where it is possible to engage in every kind of experience, only to be confronted by its exact opposite only a short distance away.

This situation also seems to apply to its architecture and the current scenario, since Naples has the capacity to have a powerful influence over any construction in contact with its resistent urban structure.

The metropolitan area has magnified every aspect and problem to huge proportions in one of the densest conurbations of the Mediterranean region, giving the impression that no municipal administration can possibly maintain complete control, and that no new building can make the slightest impression. And yet, throughout the whole 20th century, Naples was one of the capitals of an imperfect Modernism that produced buildings and districts that form the constantly changing image of the city of today.

It seems impossible to establish a fixed iconic image since the combination of high and low, humble and refined, traditional and modern, cohabit in an uneasy fusion without ever attempting to find a true equilibrium.

The generation of the "maestri" in the post-war years, such as Marcello Canino, Carlo Cocchia, Michele Capobianco, Giulio De Luca, Luigi Cosenza, Francesco di Salvo and Stefania Filo Speziale consolidated Naples' modern urban image helping to create the model of a city associated with the economical boom and frenetic growth of its residential areas.

A second generation of designers was active in the contradictory period between the Seventies and Nineties with their unashamedly Brutalist and Modernist buildings, necessary for a visual and symbolic contrast in this explosive metropolis. Architecture by Aldo Loris Rossi, Massimo Pica Ciamarra, Salvatore Bisogni and Nicola Pagliara, plus the cultural centrality of Renato de Fusco, Benedetto Gravagnuolo and Cesare de Seta, bear witness to experimentation in modern design between Brutalism and Post-Modernism whose character was expressed above all by an almost "lunar" reading of the core of Naples rather than by the influence of international debate, even though, each time, new designs demonstrated a perfectly conscious and informed awareness of global contexts and trends.

A marginal but important role was played by Francesco Venezia, whose apparent laterality (despite his important residential project for the Piazza in San Pietro a Patierno and a series of more recent museum staging designs) reveals his undeniable cultural influence on new generations.

The scenario of the last twenty years illustrates the problems, non only in Naples but throughout the country, in giving new architects opportunities to intervene in a substantial manner in urban areas that seem increasingly more indifferent to quality and merit in public architecture. The efforts of these designers is expressed by focussing maximum attention on single buildings and structures, knowing that city will then overpower them with its usual influence.

This refers to an ancient awareness is a form of expression and project strategy clearly seen in the works of Cherubino Gambardella, probably the most mature and complete architect currently present in Naples, and many of his students from the new "Luigi Vanvitelli" Architectural faculty, who are devising a third route, between modernity and traditional architecture.

The renowned architectural faculty at the Federico II University has produced designers like Roberta Amirante, Carmine Piscopo, Nicola Flora, Paolo Giardiello, Ferruccio Izzo and Giovanni Multari, who have intervened in different roles and positions on a range of smaller projects around the city.

The apparently "minor" scale of all these interventions are due to local economic instability, but also because of the conviction that it is precisely through these smaller structures that it is possible to have an influence on the living reality of Naples. Projects involving different associations at Secondigliano launched by the Municipality, parallel with the slow demolition of the Sails of Scampia, is an example of this policy, just as, on a different scale, is the impressive project by Antonio Martiniello with the Made in Cloister Foundation at Santa Caterina in Formiello.

In the background is a landscape of just a few, great, internationally renowned designs, like the series of Metropolitan Stations which has reinforced even further the relationship that Naples established after the war between contemporary art and architecture.

But it is the large urban areas that continue to represent the severe unresolved problems in the city, especially in the vast triangular expanse between the ex-industrial zones to the east of Naples, Bagnoli and the San Paolo stadium to the west, and the massive residential area to the north between Secondigliano and Piscinola.

These are the true challenges for the future of the city, opportunities but also millstones, for a political, economical and social future that seems almost impossible, despite the creative and entrepreneurial potential that Naples has demonstrated for centuries.

* Luca Molinari is a curator and writer alongside his academic career and research activities. He teaches History of Contemporary Architecture in Naples, Rome and Modena. He has written for, and still collaborates, writing for Italian and international publications.

Nuovo Policlinico

Hotel NH (Società Cattolica
di Assicurazioni Skyscraper)

azza Municipio

Hotel Romeo

Stazione Marittima

Central Station

Spaccanapoli

Chiesa di Santa Chiara

Strategies for visiting Naples

Visitors who would like to gain some knowledge of the main historical buildings and the better-known examples of modern and contemporary architecture in Naples, should calculate about a week to visit.

The itineraries A and B, in particular, require about 2 days each; the first visits the most ancient part of the city, which is very rich in historic buildings, but also includes a number of modern and contemporary structures, while the second tour is mainly composed of late 19th century and early 20th century architecture.

Each of the remaining three itineraries can be covered in a day, although the schedule will be tightly packed. Tours C and D cover a vast area that require travel by public transport and cannot be entirely visited on foot, as is possible for tour A, and most of B and E.

Itinerary A / City Centre

This itinerary begins on the seafront at the imposing 13th century **Castel dell'Ovo/01**, winding through the oldest parts of the city, very rich in ancient churches and other historical buildings, although the itinerary touches on only a few. Buildings that must not be missed are the **Duomo/20**, **Castel Nuovo (Maschio Angioino)/03** and a range of urban spaces of historical, artistic and environmental importance, such as the area of Piazza Trieste and Trento and Piazza Plebiscito with the **Galleria Umberto I/06** and the **Palazzo Reale/02**. The tour moves on to the Greek-Roman area with **Piazza del Gesù Nuovo/17**, **Piazza San Domenico/18** and **Piazza San Gaetano/19**. Contemporary architecture can be seen in the new Metro stations: (**"Municipio"/05**, **"Toledo"/10**, **"Dante"/16**, **"Museo"**) and the restored **Montesanto Station/15**. Worth a visit is **Rione Carità/11** administrative centre that dates from the late 1930s, with its most famous building, **Post Office Building/12**.

Itinerary B / Chiaia – Posillipo – Vomero

The second itinerary winds through the "bourgeois" part of the city. After a walk along the sea front and through the **Villa Comunale/25** park, at Chiaia, there is an interesting tour among neighbourhoods with Liberty and late Neapolitan eclectic architecture, located between Via Filangieri, Via dei Mille, Piazza Amedeo and **Via del Parco Margherita/30** with most of the major buildings in the lower part (especially **Palazzo Mannajuolo/27**) and villas and small apartment buildings in the streets higher up the hill. At Vomero, visit Villa Floridiana and its lovely park, and do not miss the **Certosa di San Martino/34** and the Castel Sant'Elmo, which dominate the city from above. From Posillipo, enjoy the views of the sea and the beautiful 20th century houses overlooking the Bay, especially the fine architectural examples of **Villa Crespi/40**, **Villa Oro/41**, and Villa Savarese.

Itinerary C / Fuorigrotta – Bagnoli – West Naples

The area covered by this itinerary is the zone west of the Posillipo Hill, including the Phlegrean area. Much of this route is focussed in the Fuorigrotta quarter, with a visit to the **Monte Sant'Angelo University Campus/ 52**, the **Engineering Faculty/47**, and the large area of the **Mostra d'Oltremare/45** as well as other interesting contemporary works like **The Space Cinema/44** and the CNR complex (**CNR Institute for Research on Engines/48** and **New Technological Centre/49**). Close by, at Bagnoli, is the **Città della Scienza/42** on the edge of a vast industrial area which has been awaiting redevelopment for many years. This lies on the border with the districts of **Quarto Municipal Agreement Housing Complex/54** and Pozzuoli, where visitors can admire the refined restoration project of the **Cathedral Temple/55** and the elegant design of the **Olivetti Factory/56**.

Itinerary D / North Naples

The itinerary covers all the northern quarters of the city, with two tours outside the city perimeter: to Casoria for the **Office Building/64** and above all, to Afragola to view the new **High Speed Railway Station/65**, designed by Zaha Hadid. From here, the tour takes the direction of the hospital complex in the hills, with the **CE.IN.GE. – International Centre for Genetic Engineering/59** and the **Palazzina Cosenza/58** designed by the famous Neapolitan architect, Cosenza, restored by Od'A architects. The itinerary continues through the northern outskirts where there are several residential complexes from different periods: the **Residential Complex in Chiaiano/60**, **Social housing complex in Piscinola/61**, **Residential Complex in Marianella/62** and the notoriously famous **Scampia Sails complex/63**. The tour concludes near the **Capodichino Airport/67** at the **Town Hall and Residential Apartments in San Pietro a Patierno/66** by Francesco Venezia, terminating in Capodimonte, with its magnificent **Reggia/69** and famous park.

Itinerary E / East Naples

This itinerary visits the zone immediately to the east of the ancient city centre, part of the imposing **Real Albergo dei Poveri/71** redesigned by Ferdinando Fuga in the 18th century, and abandoned today. The tour continues to the modern **Naples Administration District/73** , to reach the **Central Station/75** and the new **"Garibaldi" Metro Station/76** . From here, it moves towards the port, where two of the most interesting examples of 20th century Neapolitan architecture are located: the **Fish Market/78** by Luigi Cosenza and the **Casa del Portuale/79** by Aldo Loris Rossi. In the former industrial area further to the east there are two recent redevelopment interventions: the **Brin69/80**, and the **San Giovanni Campus at the University of Naples Federico II/81**.

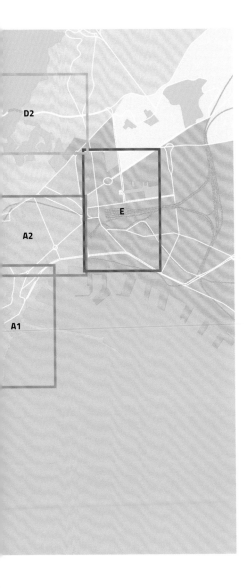

Routes

A. City Centre
B. Chiaia – Posillipo –
Vomero
C. Fuorigrotta – Bagnoli –
West Naples
D. North Naples
E. East Naples

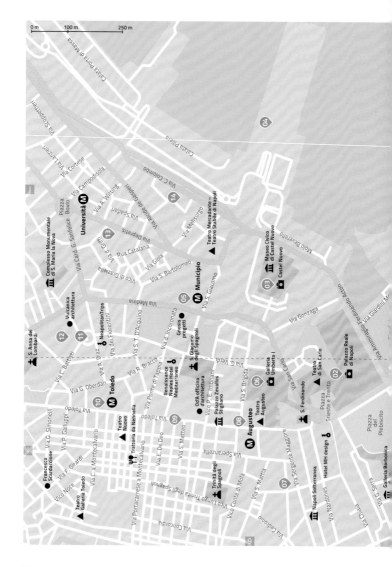

0 m   100 m   250 m

Calata Porta di Massa

Via Scopettieri

Via Cortese

Via Lanzieri

Piazza Bovio

Via A. Wirting

Via C. Colombo

Via Abate de Gasperi

Università Ⓜ

Via Spaderi

Via Campodisola

Via Depretis

Calata Piliero

🏛 Complesso Monumentale di S. Maria la Nova

Via Card. G. Sanfelice

Rua Catalana

Via A. Grifi

13

Via Gioia

04

Via Melisurgo

Via S. Bartolomeo

🏛 S. Anna dei Lombardi

Via C. Battisti

12

11

🛆 Vulcanica architettura

Vico di Grazzella

🏛 Teatro Mercadante – Teatro Stabile di Napoli

▲

🍴 NeapolitanTrips

Via A. Diaz

Via S. T. D'Aquino

Via d. Incoronata

Via Medina

Ⓜ Municipio

Via S. Giacomo

Molo Beverello

🏛 Museo Civico di Castel Nuovo

03

▲ Castel Nuovo

Via Gonzaga

Via Giardini

Via dell'Ammiraglio Ferdinando Acton

🍴 Gnosis progetti

05

🛆 OdA officina d'architettura

Via R. Bracco

Via Ponte di Tappia

Via G. Oberdan

🏛 S. Giacomo degli Spagnoli

🍴 Renaissance Naples Hotel Mediterraneo

Via P. E. Imbriani

🛆 Palazzo Zevallos Stigliano

Via G. Verdi

🛆 Galleria Umberto I

06

Via S. Brigida

Via San Carlo

🛆 Teatro di San Carlo

🛆 Palazzo Reale di Napoli

02

🍴 Francesco Scardaccione

Via G. Simonelli

Via P. Galluppi

Via Toledo

Ⓜ Toledo

10

Via C.a Montecalvario

🍴 Trattoria da Nennella

Teatro Nuovo

Via Toledo

Via E. De Deo

Via S. Matteo

09

Ⓜ Augusteo

08

🛆 Teatro Augusteo

🏛 S. Ferdinando

Piazza Trieste e Trento

07

Vico Lungo Trinità degli Spagnoli

Teatro Galleria Toledo

▲

Vico Noce

Vico F. Girardi

Via Portacarrese a Montecalvario

🏛 Trinità degli Spagnoli

Via Speranzella

Via Sergente Maggiore

Via Conte di Mola

Via S. Mattia

🍴 Hotel MH design

🏛 Napoli Sotterranea

Via Nardones

Piazza del Plebiscito

Via Cedronio

Via S. Serra

Via Chiaia

🏛 Galleria Borbonica

Via Concordia

6

26

City Centre

01. Castel dell'Ovo
02. Palazzo Reale
03. Castel Nuovo (Maschio Angioino)
04. Stazione Marittima
05. "Municipio" Metro Station
06. Galleria Umberto I
07. Market and Community Centre in the Quartieri Spagnoli
08. Cinema teatro Augusteo
09. Banco di Napoli Headquarters
10. "Toledo" Metro Station
11. Rione Carità
12. Post Office Building
13. Telephone Company Building
14. Hotel Romeo (ex Flotta Lauro Building)

City Centre

0 m   100 m   250 m

21 🏛 Museo Madre

Vico Longo

Via Domenico Cirillo

Via Carbonara

Vico Venezia

✝ S. Francesco

Piazza
Enrico de Nicola

Via Carriera Grande

🍴 Mimì alla
Ferrovia

ettembrini

Via Loffredi

Via Santi Apostoli

Via O. Costa

22
📷 Castel
Capuano

Via A. Poerio

🏛 Complesso
Monumentale
Donnaregina

✝ S. Giuseppe
dei Ruffi

Via P. Trinchera

Via C. Muzii

📷 Palazzo
Arcivescovile

20
✝ Duomo
di Napoli

Via dei Tribunali

Via S. Maria a Cancello

Via S. Giuseppe Calasanzio

tticaglia

🏛 Museo del Tesoro
di San Gennaro

✝ S. Maria
ad Agnone

Vico dei Giganti

Vico Scassacocchi

Via delle Zite

Via M. Postica

✝ Santissima
Annunziata

✝ S. Pietro
ad Aram

Paolo
giore ✝

✝ S. Lorenzo
Maggiore

Via P. Colletta

Via dell'Annunziata

8

19
🏛 Museo di
San Lorenzo
Maggiore

Via Vicaria Vecchia

Via S. Arcangelo a Baiano

Ⓗ Ospedale
Cardinale
Ascalesi

Via Nolana

✝ S. Gregorio
Armeno

Via Duomo

🏛 Archivio
di Stato

🏛 Museo Civico
Gaetano Filangieri

✝ S. Agostino
della Zecca

Via B. Chioccarelli

Via G. Savarese

San Biagio dei Librai

Via del Grande Archivio

Via dei Cimbri

Corso Umberto I

Via G. Mattei

Via di Lavinaio

✝ S. Severino
e Sossio

Via Capasso

Santi Filippo
e Giacomo ✝

Via Starace

Via Bianchini

Via Duca di S. Donato

Piazza
S. Eligio

23
Piazza
Mercato

✝ S. Maria
del Carmine

Giovanni Paladino

🏛 Museo di
Paleontologia

Via Mancini

Corso Umberto I

Via Duomo

Rua Francesca

✝ S. Eligio
Maggiore

Piazza
del Carmine

seo
eologia

📷 Università degli
Studi di Napoli
Federico II

Via Scialoia

Via Ciccone Fossataro

Piazza
Masaniello

Via Grande degli Orefici

Via Marotta

Via Capece

Calata Villa del Popolo

Via Nuova Marina

Calata Villa del popolo

J

Via Porta di Massa

Via Lanzieri

Via Soppettieri

Autorità
Portuale
di Napoli

9

ersità

K

29

01. Castel dell'Ovo

Via Eldorado 3
80132, Naples

Summer
Mon - Sat / 9 am - 7.30 pm
Sun / 9 am - 2 pm
Winter
Mon - Sat / 9 am - 6.30 pm
Sun / 9 am - 2 pm

+39 081 7954592
casteldellovo@comune.napoli.it
www.comune.napoli.it/
casteldellovo

 Funicolare Centrale >
Augusteo

A famous legend relates that the name of the castle (Egg Castle) originates with the story that Virgil hid an egg in a cage in the castle foundations and that, if the egg was ever broken, this would bring disaster to the city. The current castle was built in Norman times on the ruins of former fortifications on the island of Megaride, which in Roman times was the site of the magnificent villa of Lucullus, but even earlier, the ancient origins of Parthenope. Under Frederick II, the castle was transformed into a royal residence and housed the crown treasures. It was almost completely destroyed in 1503, but was rebuilt several times over successive centuries; in 1975, important restoration work reinstated it as a public building after its bad decline in the 17th and 18th centuries.

Today the castle has many functions, including being home to the Campana section of the Museo di Etnopreistoria of the Italian Alpine Association, as well as hosting other exhibitions. In its wonderful position jutting out to sea, the castle terraces offer magnificent views of the seafront, the city skyline and the gulf of Naples.

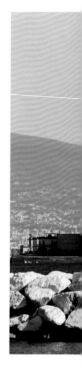

© Archivio Comune di Napoli

© Giuliana Vespere

architects	type	construction
-	museum, offices	12th century

02. Palazzo Reale

Piazza del Plebiscito 1
80132, Naples

Thu - Tue / 9 am - 8 pm
Wen / closed

+39 081 5808255
pm-cam.palazzoreale.napoli@
beniculturali.it
www.polomusealecampania.
beniculturali.it

 1 > Municipio

 Funicolare Centrale >
Augusteo

The Palace is set in the very famous Piazza del Plebiscito, formerly the entrance to the Palace. The piazza owes its current theatrical aspect to the completion of the palace by the Prince of Salerno in the 18th century, and to the Prefecture built in the early 19th century, but above all, to the church and colonade of San Francesco di Paola (1846).

The palace was begun in the early 17th century, and was designed by Domenico Fontana, but was altered and extended several times over the centuries. The façade with its three architectural orders dates back to the original project, but in the late 19th century, Umberto I added a metopa bearing the royal coat of arms, and statues of the kings of Naples set in the ground floor niches created by Vanvitelli in the 18th century.

The Palace houses the Superintendence of Architectural and Archaeological Heritage and the National Library, as well as the Museum of the Palace's Royal apartments. Visitors can view rooms with original decorations and furnishings, as well as the Monumental Staircase and the Royal Chapel by Francesco Antonio Picchiatti, and the Court theatre by Ferdinando Fuga.

Giuliana Vechbia

architects
Domenico Fontana

type
museum, offices

construction
1616

03. Castel Nuovo (Maschio Angioino)

Via Vittorio Emanuele III
80133, Naples

Mon – Sat / 8.30 am - 7 pm
Sun / closed

+39 081 7957709
patrimonio.artistico.
beniculturali@comune.napoli.it
www.comune.napoli.it

 1 > Municipio

 Funicolare Centrale >
Augusteo

The imposing mass of Castel Nuovo, or Maschio Angioino as it is more commonly and mistakenly known, sits overlooking the port and the main harbour. Today, following centuries of fires and decay, of the former Angevin royal residence (1279-1284) only the Palatine chapel remains, while the rest of the fortress was rebuilt on the same site by Alfonso V of Aragon in the 15th century, using Catalan builders and craftsmen.

The trapezoidal plan features five cylindrical towers crowned with merlons rising above a massive base set into the cliff. A monumental entrance arch, inspired by the Roman triumphal arches, was erected between 1453 and 1468, and leads to a courtyard and a large external staircase, typical of 15th century Catalan architecture. At the top of the stairs is the Hall of the Barons, with a magnificent ribbed vault, and which, today, hosts the Municipal City Council. Following its history as the centre of Angevin, Aragonese and Bourbon rule, today the castle belongs to the Municipality and, as well as the City Council Hall, it also houses the Civic Museum and the Neapolitan Society of Homeland History.

© Archivio Comune di Napoli

© Giulietta Vespere

architects	type	construction
-	museum, offices	1284 / 1479

04. Stazione Marittima

Piazzale della Stazione Marittima, Molo Angionino
80133, Naples

open to the public

+39 081 5514448
info@terminalnapoli.it
www.terminalnapoli.it

 1 > Municipio

The construction of a new maritime station became part of the regime's programme of turning Naples into the "Port of the Empire," the greatest seaport of the Mediterranean Sea. The project was entrusted to Cesare Bazzani, a member of the Royal Academy of Italy, who in 1933, after a rather questionable selection process, won a call issued by the Ministry of Public Works.

Bazzani fulfilled the tender requirements by designing a transversal "bridge" structure supported at first floor level by two side wings, 180 metres long. The construction gave the impression of a gateway to the city, framed on one side by the hill of San Martino and the silhouette of Vesuvius on the other. On the façade facing the city are two clock towers which, although not excessively tall, heighten the building which would otherwise seem compressed because of its strongly horizontal form. The towers provide a more dignified and monumental effect.

© CLEAN Edizioni

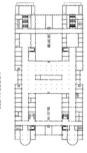

© CLEAN Edizioni

architects
Cesare Bazzani

type
maritime station

construction
1936

05. "Municipio" Metro Station

Piazza del Municipio
80133, Naples

open to the public

+39 800 639525
info@anm.it
www.anm.it

 1 > Municipio

The construction of this strategic station, the hub for metropolitan railway lines 1 and 6, was subject to very long delays because of the exceptional archaeological finds discovered during excavation work, which also led to numerous changes in the initial project design.

From the beginning, the concept was based on a dialogue between the previous structures and the use of pure austere lines, clad in lava stone and a white plaster finish. The final version is aimed at highlighting part of the ancient structures which were discovered, including the ruins of the archaic port of Neapolis and the foundations of the external Angevin defence walls at Castel Nuovo, like the Molo and Incoronata fortified towers.

The upper part was completed in 2015, with the upgrading of the area in front of the Palazzo San Giacomo around the Neptune Fountain (by famous artists like Domenico Fontana, Michelangelo Naccherino, Pietro Bernini, Cosimo Fanzago) and the opening of the line 1 station below. Work continues for the opening up of the line 6 station and the upgrading of the piazza facing the seafront.

© Studio DAZ

© Giacomo Visconti

architects
Alvaro Siza, Eduardo Souto
de Moura, Studio DAZ

type
station, public space

construction
2015

06. Galleria Umberto I

Via Toledo, Via Santa Brigida, Via Giuseppe Verdi, Via San Carlo
80132, Naples

open to the public

 1 > Municipio

 Funicolare Centrale > Augusteo

The construction of the Galleria was part of the plan to redevelop the Santa Brigida area, and was one of the most important urban development projects of the late 19th century, destined to change the layout of one of the nerve centres of the city forever. The area had been the focus of several projects in previous decades, and had been redefined with the demolition of existing decrepit buildings, and the construction of four large buildings in Neo-Renaissance style with Serlian and mullioned windows, plaster work, and statues in niches, designed by Emmanuele Rocco with the collaboration of Antonio Curri and Ernesto Di Mauro. The four buildings enclose the pre-existent churches of Santa Brigida and San Ferdinando, and surround a vast central arcade roofed in iron and glass, with a high central dome designed by Paolo Boubèe. Because of the business and commercial importance of the area, the galleria was constructed within a very short time compared to building standards of the period. It was inaugurated in 1892, and immediately became the centre of Neapolitan cultural and social life as well as a symbol of modernity.

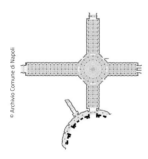

Giuliana Vespere

architects
Paolo Boubèe, Emmanuele
Rocco, Antonio Curri, Ernesto
Di Mauro

type
public space, residential,
retail, offices

construction
1892

07. Market and Community Centre in the Quartieri Spagnoli

Via Sergente Maggiore, Vico Tiratoio
80132, Naples

external viewing only

 1 > Municipio

 Funicolare Centrale > Augusteo

This market with an incorporated community centre designed by Salvatore Bisogni and Anna Buonaiuto, is a very rare case of the integration of a modern building within the web of 16th century streets in the Quartieri Spagnoli (Spanish Quarters). The plot was the previous site of a church which had collapsed, and the land was donated by the Waldesian Community to the Municipality of Naples in the 1980s, to build a structure for the service of the local community. It was built twenty years later and inaugurated in 2001. It is composed of eight stores on the lower floor and ten on the upper floor, built around a central courtyard, and another 3-storey masonry building in Rationalist style, with a loggia and terrace open towards the street for social activities. The complex was used for only a few months after it was opened, and was then abandoned. The market still functions in the external areas in the surrounding narrow streets.

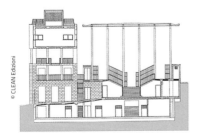

© CLEAN Edizioni

architects
Salvatore Bisogni,
Anna Buonaiuto

type
retail

construction
2001

08. Cinema teatro Augusteo

Piazzetta Duca d'Aosta
80132, Naples

open to the public only
during specific events

+39 081 414243
teatroaugusteo@libero.it
www.teatroaugusteo.it

 1 > Municipio

 Funicolare Centrale >
Augusteo

This building, which is highly emblematic of the spirit of its time, overlooks a small piazza almost opposite the entrance to Galleria Umberto I from Via Toledo. The academically classical façade designed by Arnaldo Foschini, and the decorations clearly influenced by the style of the late 19th century, are in contrast with two examples of modernism concealed within the building: the first is the lower station of the central funicular railway (the third built in Naples after those of Chiaia (1889) and Montesanto (1891) which was completed in 1928 under the supervision of the Government High Commission. The other modernist feature is the daring reinforced concrete roof, 30 metres in diameter, designed by Pier Luigi Nervi. It is unanimously considered as the first important structure by the young engineer, which incorporated the seeds of several structural and figurative aspects he was to introduce later in many of his construction designs.
The cinema, now used exclusively as a theatre, has a traditional layout, with four rows of loges and a dress circle, and is renowned for the technological solutions, considered innovative for their time.

© Giuliana Vespere

architects
Arnaldo Foschini,
Pier Luigi Nervi

type
theatre

construction
1929

09. Banco di Napoli Headquarters

Via Toledo 177 - 178
80132, Naples

partly open to the public

+39 081 7921111

 1 > Municipio, Toledo

Funicolare Centrale >
Augusteo

The building was designed by Marcello Piacentini and built in 1939 to celebrate the fourth centenary of the founding of the Banco di Napoli.

The Roman architect decided to set the building back from the street front to emphasise its monumental impact and to improve the perspective view. The main façade is divided into three levels separated by string courses. The base plinth is in grey stone with two rows of rectangular windows. The intermediate section is in travertine with two floors of large arched openings, crowned by an architrave section, set back slightly from the cornice, and punctuated by a series of small openings. The marble surface is divided by long vertical incisions to mark the window openings and add interest to the façade. In 1986, Nicola Pagliara designed a series of pools, planters and seating along the length of the plinth base, while more recently, Michele De Lucchi modernised the atrium and large, triple-height hall which is lit from above by a vast skylight.

architects
Marcello Piacentini

type
offices

construction
1939

10. "Toledo" Metro Station

Via Toledo, Via Armando Diaz
80134, Naples

open to the public

+39 800 639525
info@anm.it
www.anm.it

 1 > Toledo

This station is strategically important because of its position in the heart of the city centre, and is renowned for the natural elements incorporated in its design; it is characterised by the great *lumière cannon* covered in blue glass tiles that penetrates the depths from the external road surface as far as the escalators of the final mezzanine level and from particular lining that with its various shades of colour, transitions from the yellow tones of the upper levels to the blue tones that characterises the areas below sea level. The last corridor, designed by Bill Wilson, is flanked by two long images of water and its wall and floor surfaces are entirely covered in blue, accentuating the passengers' impression of going deep underwater.

On surface level, the entire area at the crossroads between Via Toledo and Via Diaz has been transformed into a pedestrian square with new urban furnishing and seating.

The station has been awarded a number of prizes (including Europe's most beautiful subway station, by the Daily Telegraph in 2012) bearing witness to the great success achieved by the Neapolitan subway system, even in the press.

 © Oscar Tusquets Blanca

© Andrea Resmini

architects
Oscar Tusquets Blanca

type
station, public space

construction
2012

11. Rione Carità

**Piazza Giacomo Matteotti,
Via Cesare Battisti,
Via Armando Diaz,
Via Toledo**
80133 - 80134, Naples

open to the public

 1 > Toledo

The eradication of this area to create a new business centre involved the destruction of several blocks of the historic urban fabric including the churches of San Giuseppe Maggiore, San Tommaso d'Aquino and Fiorentini, as well as the oldest theatre in the city.
The trite Fascist regime rhetoric that characterised the style of many buildings, was countered by a few of the best architects of the time, who experimented with interesting projects, in a compromise between the unavoidable monumental design and the experiments in European classicist rationalism of the same period. The most successful were Vaccaro and Franzi, with their iconic Post Office Building (see p. 52), but also Canino with his Palazzo degli Uffici Finanziari (1937), inspired by Nordic Classicism; the huge building is clad with narrow bricks and mitigated by concave and convex structures on the opposite façades.
Among other outstanding buildings are the Palazzo della Provincia (1936) by Canino and Chiaromonte, a triumph in travertine stone and klinker with a richly decorated bronzed portal, and the Casa del Mutilato (1940) by Camillo Guerra, in perfect "Fascist style" featuring a vast portal and an orderly series of gigantic pillars.

architects
various

type
residential, retail, offices

construction
1936 - 1941

12. Post Office Building

Piazza Giacomo Matteotti 2
80133, Naples

partly open to the public

+39 081 5524410

 1 > Toledo

An example of very fine architecture in the new Rione Carità quarter, the Post Office Building is located on a complex site: an irregular shape, with a strong difference in ground level, and in close proximity to examples of traditional architecture. After winning the contract competition proposing a historicist solution, the architects changed direction with a project that while very modern, still maintained its monumental aspect, adding distinction to the new business district.

The pure, well-proportioned, front curved façade, acts as a backdrop for the piazza and its iconic element, providing a glimpse of the building's purpose, with large openings on the ground floor halls for the public, regular rows of rectangular windows on the two upper floors housing the office spaces, and a continuous strip of windows underlining the cornice that formerly housed the telegraph equipment. The immense glazed entrance portal, divided by a massive pillar, clearly shows the triple height of the foyer.

The façades of the building, smooth, without protruding elements, are clad in quality stone: dark Baveno diorite stone for the plinth base, and light Vallestrona marble for the upper floors.

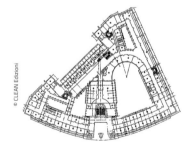

© CLEAN Edizioni

© Giuliana Vespere

architects
Giuseppe Vaccaro, Gino Franzi

type
offices

construction
1936

13. Telephone Company Building

Via Agostino Depretis 40
80133, Naples

external viewing only

 1 > Università

This was the third building designed by Camillo Guerra for the telephone company while working for the civil engineering technical office, following the building erected in Via Crispi, inspired by 17th century Neapolitan architecture, and the other in Piazza Nolana, in a much plainer style, near the Wagnerschule.

The building in Via Depretis, completed in 1925, and then bombed during the war, was rebuilt between 1945 and 1946, once again to Guerra's design. It was based on a similar layout, but the external design was somewhat different, with historic references combined with a more dramatic effect.

The façade is dominated by a huge portal, set under a large tympanun that occupies the entire central segment. On each side, the façade is clearly divided into three horizontal sections: a plinth base in piperno stone with arched windows, a centre section with tall paired columns that frame the recessed openings, and an upper section, with a double order of square windows crowned by an imposing neo-Renaissance style cornice.

architects
Camillo Guerra

type
offices

construction
1946

14. Hotel Romeo (ex Flotta Lauro Building)

Via Cristoforo Colombo 45
80133, Naples

open to the public

+39 081 6041580
welcome@romeohotel.it
www.romeohotel.it/naples/it

 1 > Municipio

The original building was designed by Antonio Scivittaro for the offices of the Neapolitan shipping magnate, Achille Lauro, in 1950. It was composed of a double-level plinth base faced in marble, supporting a clean-lined projecting structure, 7 storeys high, completely faced in glass interrupted only by fine horizontal string courses.
The refurbishing project was designed by Kenzo Tange and constructed by the firm of his son Paul, who has transformed the office building into a luxury hotel with views over the port. It has 82 rooms, two restaurants, a wellness centre covering 1,000 square metres, and an external panoramic swimming pool. The intervention by the Japanese firm was completed in 2008, with the radical transformation of the internal spaces with luxury finishes, and a glass façade overlooking Via Cristoforo Colombo. This was aimed at emphasising the transparent effect of the upper structure while modifying the original simple design. The white platform roof echoes that designed by Scivittaro but never built.

© Giuseppa Vespa

architects
Antonio Scivittaro /
Tange Associates

type
hotel

construction
1950 / 2008

15. Montesanto Station

Piazza Montesanto
80135, Naples

open to the public

2 > Montesanto

**Cumana /
Circumflegrea /
Funicolare di
Montesanto** >
Montesanto

The station built in 1889 and restructured several times, groups the terminals of the Cumana and Circumflegrea railway lines that connect Naples with Campi Flegrei, and the lower station of the Vomero funicular railway. The core of the two storey complex is the hall set between two plastered structures with ashlar stone corner work; the ground floor colonnade opens onto the busy Piazza di Montesanto and houses the ticket offices and stores, while the railway platforms are accessed on the first floor by a terrace with glass roofing supported by fine cast iron pillars.

The redevelopment project achieved an excellent balance between the restoration of the original building while incorporating clearly modern elements which are integrated with the adjacent piazza. The new elements that surround the hall, have a strongly technological impact, especially the structure on the Via Olivella side that houses the funicular station, faced completely with *brise-soleil* louvres. The platform area has been renovated and decorated with photos by Mimmo Jodice portraying the beauty of the Campi Flegrei; new light and airy glass roofing provides overhead lighting.

© Silvio d'Ascia Architecture

© Barbara Jodice

architects	type	construction
Antonio Liotta / Silvio d'Ascia	station	1889 / 2010

16. "Dante" Metro Station

Piazza Dante
80135, Naples

open to the public

+39 800 639525
info@anm.it
www.anm.it

 1 > Dante

This project by Gae Aulenti was one of the first of the city's Metropolitan Railway Art Stations, and incorporated the redesigning of the 18th century Piazza by Luigi Vanvitelli, built over the historic Largo del Mercatello.

At street level, the only signs of the subway station are two glazed structures that protect the stairs and elevators set on each side of the statue of Dante Alighieri. The remaining piazza area is a vast and anonymous, completely pedestrian space, paved with volcanic stone, in front of the symmetrical semi-circular façade by Vanvitelli.

Underground, a series of contemporary art works are exhibited along the route leading to the railway lines. The works include Pistoletto, Kosuth and Kounellis, providing commuters with a kind of "obligatory museum", according to the clever definition by Achille Bonito Oliva.

Aulenti also designed the nearby "Museo" station, which exhibits copies of the Farnese Hercules and the Carafa horse's head; the originals are on show at the national archaeological museum, that also exhibits photographs by Jodice, D'Alessandro, Biasucci, Donato, Mariniello.

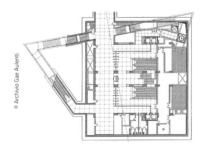

architects
Gae Aulenti

type
station, public space

construction
2002

17. Piazza del Gesù Nuovo

Piazza del Gesù Nuovo
80134, Naples

open to the public

 1 > Dante

In the centre of the piazza stands the Spire of the Immacolata, a monument erected in the mid-18th century and famous for its intricately carved marble decoration. In addition to the fascinating Pignatelli di Monteleone and Pandola palaces, the church of the Immacolata rises on the western side of the piazza. It was built on the site of the 15th century Palazzo di Sanseverino di Salerno, whose ashlar stone was reused for the façade. The rich Baroque interior is based on a central plan layout with a large dome, and contains many prestigious works of art.

On the eastern side of the piazza is the Church of Santa Chiara, with its rough façade in yellow tuff stone, carved marble rose window, and pronaos in piperno stone, commissioned by Robert of Anjou in 1310, and richly embellished during the 18th century. Few of the decorations by some of the most important artists of the period, still exist, destroyed during the bombing in the Second World War. Successive restoration work uncovered the original Provençal Gothic architecture. Traces of the 18th century interventions can be seen in the famous cloister, Chiostro delle Clarisse, designed by Vaccaro and completely faced with multi-coloured majolica, designed by Giuseppe and Donato Massa.

© Giuliana Vespere

architects
-

type
public space

construction
-

18. Piazza San Domenico Maggiore

Piazza San Domenico Maggiore
80134, Naples

open to the public

 1 > Dante

This piazza is among the most important in the old city centre, and is surrounded by prominent buildings including the Corigliano, Casacalenda and Petrucci palaces; in the centre is the spire of San Domenico, the work of famous artists such as Picchiatti, Fanzago and Vaccaro (1658-1737).

The octagonal apse of the Church of San Domenico, begun in the late 3rd century and completed in 1324, can be seen from the piazza, while the façade, showing clear evidence of different successive architectural styles, faces the opposite direction, onto a courtyard reached along a narrow street of the same name. The interior, rich in works of art, has been modified over time, and some interventions, including restoration work in the 19th century, have compromised the original aspect. The sacristy is particularly interesting: it is entirely panelled in walnut cupboards, and also includes a gallery that contains the caskets of figures linked with the court of Aragon. There is also a fine vault with frescoes by Francesco Solimena. Exhibitions and cultural events are held in the adjacent convent, which underwent important restoration work between 2000 and 2011.

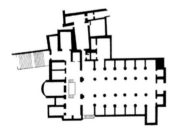

architects
-

type
public space

construction
-

19. Piazza San Gaetano

Piazza San Gaetano
80138, Naples

open to the public

 1 > Dante

The piazza is named after the bronze statue of Saint Gaetano (1737) and is built on the site of an ancient Greek agora, later the Roman forum, centre of the political and commercial life of Neapolis. It was surrounded by the macellum, the ancient market with its small shops, today preserved under the Basilica of San Lorenzo Maggiore, and the Temple of the Dioscuri. An early Christian church was built on its ruins, and later replaced by the current Church of San Paolo Maggiore.

San Lorenzo, a celebration of Neapolitan Gothic style, is one of the most complex examples of historic stratification in the old city centre. The first church was built in the 6th century, rebuilt in 1275, and transformed later in Baroque style. The Baroque façade of San Felice (1742) still remains, while the internal decorations were eliminated during 20th century restoration.

The façade of San Paolo, has two orders of grooved pilasters, and two Corinthian columns from the Roman Temple on the sides of the portal. The church was built by the Theatine order between 1583 and 1630, and has a rich interior: the sacristy and the Firrao chapel are especially fine. Close by, in Via San Gregorio, famous for its artisanal Christmas cribs, is the historic complex of San Gregorio Armeno, with its beautiful cloister.

© Giuliana Vespasi

architects
-

type
public space

construction
-

20. Duomo

Via Duomo 147
80138, Naples

Mon - Sat / 8.30 am -
12.30 pm, 4.30 pm - 7 pm
Sun / 8 am - 1.30 pm,
5 pm - 7.30 pm

+39 081 449097

 2 > Cavour

Dedicated to the Madonna Assunta, the Cathedral was built in the early 14th century on the site previously occupied by two Paleo-Christian basilicas, one of which still exists today under the present church, although it has been transformed into a beautiful Baroque interior.

The Cathedral was subject to numerous changes over the centuries: the portals date back to 1407, the carved, painted wooden ceilings are from the 12th century, and the radical transformation of the apse and the changes to the pillars in the nave were carried out in the 18th century. The current façade, designed by Errico Alvino in Neo-gothic style, was created in the second half of the 19th century.

The crypt (or Carafa Chapel, 1497), outstanding for its original composition, was perhaps designed by Bramante, to conserve the relic of Saint Gennaro, and is considered a magnificent example of Renaissance architecture.

A wonderful model of Neapolitan Baroque design is the Cappella del Tesoro (1637), with a Greek cross plan and large dome, created by artists such as Cosimo Fanzago, il Domenichino, lo Spagnoletto, Giovanni Lanfranco.

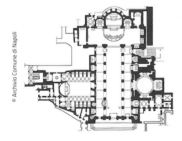

© Archivio Comune di Napoli

Giuliana Vespere

architects	type	construction
-	church	1313 / 1905

21. Madre Museum

Via Luigi Settembrini 79
80139, Naples

Mon - Sat / 10 am - 7.30 pm
Sun / 10 am - 8 pm
Tue / closed

+39 081 19737254
info@madrenapoli.it
www.madrenapoli.it

 2 > Cavour

The museum, whose initials stand for Museo di Arte Contemporanea Donnaregina (Madre), takes its name from the palace where it is housed, the 19th century Palazzo Donnaregina. After restoration in 1980, the building was left unoccupied following bad damage from flooding in 2001. It was later purchased by the Regione Campania, who granted use of the building to the Fondazione Donnaregina as a contemporary art museum.

The restoration and conversion work of the entire palace was performed by Alvaro Siza with the collaboration of Studio DAZ. Siza wished to respect the historic nature of the building as far as possible, and maintained a clean simple décor, particularly suited to house many site specific works created for the museum by important international artists. As well as the exhibition spaces, the 7,200 square metre building also houses a library, a media library, an auditorium, a bookshop-café area and educational workshops.

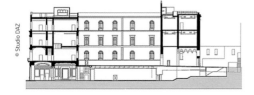

© Studio DAZ

© Martin Devrient

architects
Alvaro Siza, Studio DAZ

type
museum

construction
2007

22. Castel Capuano and Porta Capuana

Piazza Enrico de Nicola
80139, Naples

partly open to the public

1 / 2 > Garibaldi

Circumvesuviana >
Napoli Garibaldi

Established by the Normans as a defence outpost, Castel Capuano was used as an Angevin and Aragonese palace until it was transformed in 1540 by the viceroy, who converted it into a Hall of Justice, a role it maintained almost until the present day. The main façade, in line with the ancient decumanus, is fronted with a tower bearing the arms of Charles V, and the House of Habsburg.

On the other side, facing Piazza Enrico de Nicola, the castle overlooks Porta Capuana, the most important and best preserved of the ancient city gates in Naples, part of the Aragonese city walls, and one of the finest examples of 15th century military architecture. They were built to strengthen the defences of the capital and to replace the obsolete Anjou bastions. The gate was designed by Giuliano da Maiano, to echo the arch of Castel Nuovo, as an authentic triumphal arch in Carrara marble, enhanced with sculpture and high-relief carving, encased between two powerful towers in piperno stone.

The Naples Municipality is currently working to strengthen the portal and the adjacent walls to create a walking route for visitors along the city walls.

© Archivio Comune di Napoli

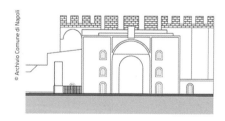

Giuliana Vespere

architects
Giuliano da Maiano

type
public space, offices

construction
Castel Capuano: 1160
Porta Capuana: 1484

23. Piazza Mercato

Piazza Mercato
80133, Naples

open to the public

 1 / 2 > Garibaldi

 Circumvesuviana >
Napoli Porta Nolana

Until 1270, the so-called Campo del Moricino was a vast open public space, predominantly used as a market place. The piazza has been the backdrop to many crucial events in Neapolitan history, including the beheading of Conradin of Swabia in 1268, the revolt led by Masaniello in 1647, and the revolution in 1799. Today it still maintains the semi-circular shape designed by Seguro in the 18th century, following a fire that destroyed the wooden shacks that housed the market.

On the western side is the Church of Sant'Eligio, built under Angevin rule, with a French Gothic style portal. Directly opposite is the Basilica del Carmine that overlooks the adjacent piazza with the same name, where the local festa del Carmine is celebrated every year on July 17. The church was completed in the early 14th century, but was radically transformed between 1755 and 1766, when it was also given a new façade. The first three orders of the bell tower (1631) were created by Giovan Giacomo di Conforto, while the octagonal steeple and pinnacle were designed by the Dominican monk, Fra' Nuvolo.

Somewhat incoherent with the piazza is the controversial Palazzo Ottieri, built in 1958 on the southern side.

© Archivio Comune di Napoli

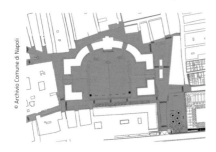

architects
Francesco Seguro

type
public space

construction
18th century

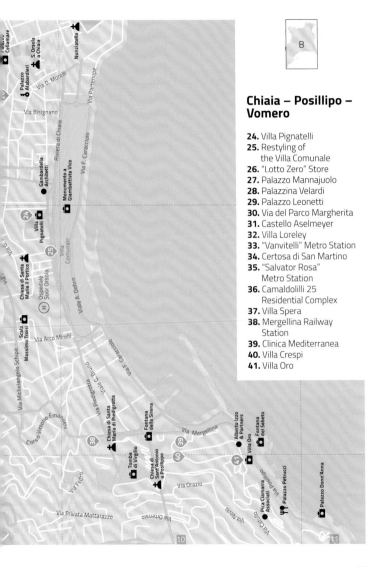

Chiaia – Posillipo – Vomero

24. Villa Pignatelli

Riviera di Chiaia 200
80121, Naples

Wen - Mon / 8.30 am - 5 pm
Tue / closed

+39 081 7612356
pm-cam.pignatelli@
beniculturali.it
www.polomusealecampania.
beniculturali.it

 2 > Piazza Amedeo

 Funicolare di Chiaia >
Parco Margherita

One of the finest examples of Neapolitan neoclassical architecture, this villa is immersed
is a small but beautiful park of rare plant
species and still maintains its original English garden layout, designed by Guglielmo
Bechi. The main façade features a magnificent Doric colonnade on the ground floor,
Ionic pilasters on the first floor, and a low
crowning pediment. Villa Pignatelli has been
home to various noble families over time:
Lord Acton who built the villa in the 1820s,
the Rothschilds, and then the Pignatelli
family, but today houses the Museo Diego
Aragona Pignatelli Cortes, composed of the
villa itself, the park, and the adjacent coach
museum. The house museum has preserved
its wonderful plaster stucco decorations,
original paintings and furniture, as well as
a prestigious collection of fine international
porcelain. The villa is also used to host temporary exhibitions and cultural events.

architects
Pietro Valente

type
museum

construction
1826

25. Restyling of the Villa Comunale

Riviera di Chiaia, Via Francesco Caracciolo, Piazza Vittoria
80121, Naples

November - April /
7 am - 10 pm
May - October /
7 am - 12 am

+39 081 7953652
assessorato.ambiente@
comune.napoli.it
www.comune.napoli.it

 2 > Piazza Amedeo

 Funicolare di Chiaia >
Parco Margherita

Inaugurated in 1781 and extended between 1807 and 1815, the "Villa Reale" was originally almost lapped by the sea. It was only later, in 1883, that the current Via Caracciolo was completed, based on the project design by Enrico Alvino.

In the late 1990s, a redevelopment scheme was launched, that involved both the planted trees and the paving. Non-natural materials were replaced with stone and rammed tuff stone. At the same time, the Atelier Mendini was responsible for the controversial restyling design, transforming the temporary, so-called "chalets" into permanent structures, clad with vibrant mosaics, to house cafés, bars, and services for the park. They also designed decorative railings with slender gilded lighting poles, an intervention that triggered strong discussions between those who supported closing the park during the night for security reasons, and those who sustained it should be open to the city at all times.

Today, the Villa is in a bad state of repair, with only a few fortunate exceptions, including the bandstand, which was recently restored by the municipal administration.

© Atelier Mendini

architects
Atelier Mendini

type
public space

construction
1999

26. "Lotto Zero" Store

Via Gaetano Filangieri 60
80121, Naples

open to the public

+39 081 2512103
infonapoli@capricapri.com
www.capricapri.com

 2 > Piazza Amedeo

 Funicolare di Chiaia >
Parco Margherita

The architect Arata managed to create this building in a particularly difficult triangular plot of only 40 square metres in Via Filangieri. Despite its limited size, it rapidly became renowned as an architectural example of its period and cultural era, as well as confirming the artistic style of the architect. The rich, imaginative, and beautifully finished decorative façade is a combination of Liberty and medieval-style references creating a successful blend of architectural and decorative elements of various origins. Intelligent research into proportions on the ground floor was able to achieve a small entrance door with a rich architrave above, alongside a wide store window to display merchandise. On the first floor is a large round arched window with a decorative border and an elegant balustrade. On the top floor are four windows divided by small double columns under the projecting balustrade of the roof terrace. Several modifications at different times have partly altered the original composition.

architects
Giulio Ulisse Arata

type
retail

construction
1912

27. Palazzo Mannajuolo

Via Gaetano Filangieri 36
80121, Naples

external viewing only

2 > Piazza Amedeo

Funicolare di Chiaia >
Parco Margherita

This building is considered one of the finest examples of Liberty architecture in the city, partly for its richly decorated exterior and partly for the refined design of the internal spaces, including the elegant oval main staircase. The building is undoubtedly the most emblematic example in the area of Via Filangieri and Via dei Mille, where Neapolitan Liberty architecture left a strong and coherent mark, especially obvious in the minor elements and the painstaking decorative detail in many buildings and similar to the large number of buildings erected in the city during expansion in the late 19th century.

The main element of the composition is the curved corner section which forms a focal point in Via dei Mille; its complex combination of solid mass and concave and convex elements, plus its crowning dome, create a definite impact at the intersection. The elaborate decorations with plaster stucco and iron elements combine to form a successful blend of Central European, Liberty, and traditional Neapolitan style, with special reference to Baroque.

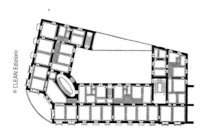

© CLEAN Edizioni

architects
Giulio Ulisse Arata

type
residential, retail, offices

construction
1911

28. Palazzina Velardi

Rampe Brancaccio 6
80132, Naples

external viewing only

 2 > Piazza Amedeo

 Funicolare di Chiaia >
Parco Margherita

This interesting residential building was designed specifically for the strongly sloping site, with steep ramps leading from Via dei Mille to Corso Vittorio Emanuele. The design was based on a play of different volumes, especially on the upper floors. Even the internal layout is perfectly adapted to the site, as are the façades that differ on each side of the building, featuring numerous openings in varying styles: single, double and triple arched windows.

The remains of the splendid early Liberty decorative elements can be seen today only in the elaborate balustrades and unusual polygonal tower on the corner, a characteristic feature of the building. However, originally, all surfaces of the building were completely decorated with plaster stucco floral and organic motifs. Another feature worthy of note is the brick and reinforced concrete attic space, technology that was decidedly innovative in Naples during that period.

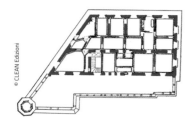

© CLEAN Edizioni

© CLEAN Edizioni

architects
Francesco De Simone

type
residential

construction
1906

29. Palazzo Leonetti

Via dei Mille 40
80121, Naples

external viewing only

2 > Piazza Amedeo

Funicolare di Chiaia >
Parco Margherita

This very large residential building, originally designed as a hotel, owes its U-shaped layout, arranged around a front garden, to careful research into the 18th century architecture of the adjacent Palazzo D'Avalos, and the desire to maintain a predominantly open aspect on the northern façade in Via dei Mille compared to the opposite side. This has created an open space for a beautiful green area visible from the street, particularly appreciated in an area where gardens are almost non-existent.

The design has a strongly classical composition, with a heavy ashlar stone plinth base, high pilaster strips along the entire façade, and typanums over the windows, but it is enhanced with floral and organic decorations and references to the Vienna Secession, with its emblematic ornamentation, in a balance between ancient and modern, typical of other works by Arata during that period.

© Andrea Nastri

architects
Giulio Ulisse Arata

type
residential, offices

construction
1910

30. Via del Parco Margherita

Via del Parco Margherita
80121, Naples

open to the public

 2 > Piazza Amedeo

 Funicolare di Chiaia >
Parco Margherita

Part of the 19th century expansion project towards the west of the city, the construction in this new street began in 1886; it led from Piazza Amedeo and wound up the hill as far as Corso Vittorio Emanuele. The commercial areas were planned in the lower areas, while the new road was designed exclusively for residential construction. Existing apartment blocks were contrasted by less intensive construction with more flexible solutions, such as private villas and smaller residential buildings. These new buildings were destined for the upper middle class, and this can be seen in the quality of the decorative elements, where the late Eclectic movement and historical symbols are combined with Liberty architecture, in an interesting blend of old and new. The result is an extremely pleasant urban environment, very harmonious as a whole despite the variety of architectural styles and different types of building.

Among the more interesting buildings are the Grand Hotel Eden (1901) by Angelo Trevisan, the Palazzina Paradisiello (1909) attributed to Giulio Ulisse Arata, Palazzo Acquaviva Coppola (1912) by the same engineer, and the small block at numbers 14-16, by Emmanuele Rocco.

© Salvatore Giordano

architects
various

type
public space

construction
1901 - 1912

31. Castello Aselmeyer

Corso Vittorio Emanuele II 166
80121, Naples

external viewing only

Funicolare di Chiaia
> Corso Vittorio
Emanuele

This picturesque residential building in dark Vesuvian stone, stands out against the light tuff stone in the hills behind it, in contrast with the surrounding scenery. It is the work of the flamboyant and visionary architect-engineer of British origin, Lamont Young, who also designed the ambitious project for Pizzofalcone, of which only the dramatic Villa Elbe remains, as well as a number of daring infrastructural and urban projects for the city of Naples.

The castle has an eclectic style with a strong English neo-Gothic influence, built to adapt to the cliff face, with crenellated towers, and openings of various forms including double arched and oval windows, lancet and rounded arch windows. Originally, Young built the castle as his personal residence calling it "Castle Lamont", but sold it later to the banker, Carlo Aselmeyer, who gave it the name it has maintained until today. Incongruous additions detract from the entrance, while the rest of the building has preserved much of its original charm, despite several alterations.

architects	**type**	**construction**
Lamont Young	residential	1902

32. Villa Loreley

Via Gioacchino Toma 14
80127, Naples

external viewing only

 1 > Vanvitelli

 **Funicolare Centrale /
Funicolare di Chiaia** >
Piazza Fuga, Cimarosa

This unusual L-shaped Liberty villa was designed specifically to sit on the corner plot of Via Toma, and is one of the major projects by Adolfo Avena, considered among the most talented Neapolitan architects of the period. The villa features a variety of architectural and design elements, as well as decorative details that freely combine Liberty and Eclectic styles, without compromising the general Anglo-American Modernist aspect of the building.

Different types of gables and cornices are set above the windows, while an interesting veranda featuring several iron flower planters alternating with masonry pillars forms one of the main elements of the composition, "hollowed out" from a corner of the building.

Inside, a very fine oval staircase was especially designed for the curved corner of the building that forms the main entrance.

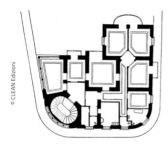

© CLEAN Edizioni

architects
Adolfo Avena

type
residential

construction
1912

33. "Vanvitelli" Metro Station

Piazza Luigi Vanvitelli
80129, Naples

open to the public

+39 800 639525
info@anm.it
www.anm.it

 1 > Vanvitelli

 **Funicolare Centrale /
Funicolare di Chiaia** >
Piazza Fuga, Cimarosa

This station is constructed completely underground and can be identified in the piazza, in the heart of the 19th-20th century Vomero quarter, only by the descending stairs and elevator. The underground space occupies almost all the same expanse as the overhead area, forming a spacious covered piazza. The station features an impressive long, vaulted, false ceiling with an explicit reference to the blue Mediterranean sky as it curves above the stairs leading to the mezzanine level.

Like most of the stations in the Neapolitan metropolitan railway system, during the re-styling work carried out in 2005, "Vanvitelli" was also transformed into an art station, with the installation of works by artists such as Vettor Pisani, Mario Merz, Gregorio Botta and Giulio Paolini, photographic works by Gabriele Basilico and Olivo Barbieri displayed on the walls of the entrance area, and coloured mosaics by Isabella Ducrot, along the platforms.

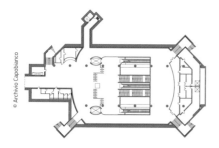

© Archivio Capobianco

© Peppe Avallone

architects
Michele Capobianco / Michele
and Lorenzo Capobianco

type
station

construction
1993 / 2005

34. Certosa di San Martino

Largo San Martino 5
80129, Naples

Mon - Tue, Thu - Sat /
8.30 am - 7.30 pm
Sun and holidays /
8.30 am - 5 pm
Wed / closed

+39 081 2294502
pm-cam.sanmartino@
beniculturali.it
www.polomusealecampania.
beniculturali.it

 1 > Vanvitelli

 Funicolare di Montesanto >
Morghen

In 1325 Tino di Camaino and Francesco De Vito were commissioned to create a religious complex at the foot of Belforte, the Angevin fortress built on the top of the Vomero Hill. Two centuries later, in 1546, Belforte was replaced by the massive Castel Sant'Elmo, with its characteristic 6-pointed star layout. Successively, during the 17th century, the Certosa was radically restored by Cosimo Fanzago, who gave the charter house its current Baroque style. The vast entrance courtyard provides a wonderful view of the Gothic pronaos of the church, with its single nave and side chapels rich in important works of art. The cloisters are particularly interesting: the Chiostro dei Procuratori, and above all, the magnificent Chiostro Grande with its central marble fountain, both designed by Dosio between the 16th and 17th centuries.

Since 1900, the Certosa has housed the Museo Nazionale di San Martino, including the Foresteria and the Quarto del Priore collections, and the famous Christmas cribs, the largest Italian collection of its kind. Magnificent panoramic views of the city and the gulf of Naples can be had from the ramparts of Castel Sant'Elmo and the Belvedere of the Certosa.

architects
Tino di Camaino, Francesco
De Vito, Attanasio Primario
/ Giovanni Antonio Dosio,
Cosimo Fanzago

type
museum

construction
1325 / 1656

35. "Salvator Rosa" Metro Station

Via Salvator Rosa
80136, Naples

open to the public

+39 800 639525
info@anm.it
www.anm.it

 1 > Salvator Rosa

The construction of this station gave rise to the redevelopment of the area located between the old narrow route climbing up to the Vomero quarter, oppressed by tall buildings, and the steep slopes crowded with high apartment buildings.

Mendini placed the station in the centre, a structure balanced between severe 20th century form and the typically ironic style of his compositions. The remains of a Roman bridge have been restored and incorporated into the surrounding area, transformed with a piazza and planted green areas, with urban furnishing elements and sculptures by artists such as Dalisi and Paladino. Along with other artists (Barisani, Rotella, Pisani, and Tatafiore), Paladino also decorated and frescoed the blind walls of the surrounding buildings to enhance the upward space as well. A mirrored steel tube containing an escalator climbs to the top of the steep slope connecting the station with the Piazza Leonardo quarter above. Mendini also designed the "Materdei" Station (2003), recognised for its colourful pinnacle and ironic urban furnishing elements. It is included in the series of Art Stations because it houses numerous works of art.

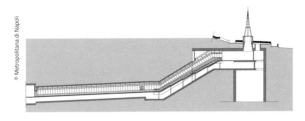

© Metropolitana di Napoli

architects
Atelier Mendini

type
station, public space

construction
2001

36. Camaldolilli 25 Residential Complex

Via Vicinale Camaldolilli 25
80128, Naples

external viewing only

🚇 **1** > Quattro Giornate

This innovative urban and environmental re-development project, based on sustainability criteria, is located within a large 11 acre green area, between Via Pigna and Via Camaldolilli, not far from the ring road and the subway.

The first intervention envisaged 23 energy class A, anti-seismic apartments, complete with terraces or private gardens and garage spaces, a condominial garden, common parking area, and a sports gym. According to the urban plan approved by the Naples city council in 2009, it will be completed with the addition of a small public park, adjacent to the De Curtis nursery and elementary school, as well as a play area for the children and a garden for the elderly. Urban vegetable plots have also been planned, together with sports facilities with swimming pool and tennis courts, which are still pending approval. A proposal has been put forward to construct a private agricultural park on the remaining land. To complete this urban and environmental redevelopment project, it has been decided to resurface the first section of Via Camaldolilli.

© Archivio OdʹA

© Archivio O...

architects
Od'A officina d'architettura

type
residential

construction
2016

37. Villa Spera

Via Torquato Tasso 615
80127, Naples

open to the public on demand

+39 081 7147301
info@antignani.biz
www.residenzedepoca.it

This villa rises alone at the top of Via Tasso; its various structural elements are designed to adapt to the natural downward slope, and the house is covered with overhanging roofing, rather unusual in Neapolitan architecture. The building is rather picturesque in nature, designed with great freedom of style, influenced by the Eclectic movement and Romanesque Revival with a range of elaborate decorative elements on each façade, but cohesive for their uniform natural stone surfaces.

Different loggias, balconies, window styles, bow-windows, and elaborate balustrades underline the architectural design, emblematic of Adolfo Avena's composition and painstaking detail throughout the building, including the suggestive interior spaces.

The villa is in excellent condition and today can be hired for events and receptions.

C31 / 181 / 627 / 681 >
Europa-Sacro Cuore

© CLEAN Edizioni

© Giuliana Vespere

architects
Adolfo Avena

type
residential, event space

construction
1922

38. Mergellina Railway Station

Corso Vittorio Emanuele II 4
80122, Naples

open to the public

www.centostazioni.it

 2 > Mergellina

Inaugurated at the same time as the Naples-Rome express railway line, this station is a fine example of symmetrical classical architecture with a travertine ashlar plinth base and an upper floor with plaster stucco decorated window frames, statues, pilasters, and columns, completed with a large arch enclosing a clock flanked by two statues. Along the main façade is a projecting shelter in cast iron with floral decorations and coloured glass roof panels.

The two atriums at each end of the building, adapted to the change in street levels, were originally destined for arrivals and departures, while the central area provided access to the restaurant. These three large spaces are covered in coffered barrel vaulted ceilings with glass block inserts, and are decorated in a sober eclectic style in a blend of neoclassical and late Liberty. A staircase gives access to the platforms set behind the building on the upper level. The station has not been used for main line railway traffic for several years, but still serves as a subway station for Campania region urban lines.

architects
Gaetano Costa

type
station

construction
1927

39. Clinica Mediterranea

Via Orazio 2
80122, Naples

open to the public

+39 081 7259690
dirsan@clinicamediterranea.it
www.clinicamediterranea.it

 2 > Mergellina

 **Funicolare
di Mergellina** >
Mergellina

This clinic is one of the most important works designed by Sirio Giametta in the context of hospital construction.

The shape and orientation of the site, confined by the steep slope and the curved corner of Via Orazio, influenced the design: the service areas, laboratories and several second class bedrooms are built along the side facing the embankment, while the private patients' rooms overlook the panoramic views. On this side of the building, with the widest view of the sea, the regular façade is interrupted by a projecting semicircular tower with large windows, housing the main entrance.

In 2015 the Gambardella architectural firm completed a total restoration of the clinic aimed at creating a reassuring and homely atmosphere for patients and families, achieving a delicate balance between the historical importance of a celebrated building and the needs and aspects of a contemporary hospital. The aim of opening up the structure to the city was obtained with the design of the entrance hall, including a bistrot, spaces for temporary exhibitions, and a covered terrace for future events and congresses.

© Gambardella Architetti

© Peppe Maisto

architects
Sirio Giametta /
Gambardella Architetti

type
hospital

construction
1945 / 2015

40. Villa Crespi

Via Felice Minucio 8
80122, Naples

external viewing only

**Funicolare
di Mergellina** >
Sant'Antonio

This villa, designed by the Polish architect, Davide Pacanowski with the expert collaboration of engineer Adriano Galli, is built on a small, very steep plot on a tuff cliff top in Posillipo, overlooking the gulf of Naples. Thanks to the daring structural design, the main block and cantilevered terraces of this home seem almost suspended in space over the bay of Mergellina below. The reinforced slabs of all three storeys of this building are supported within a single concrete "mushroom" pillar in various sections, while the other ends are embedded in the cliff face.

The façades of the different blocks of this clean Rationalist style structure are distinguished by the variation in surface finishes: tuff stone for all the façades rooted in the cliff face, and a white plaster finish for all projecting elements. The top floor, that extends out over the vast panorama, has a planted roof garden.

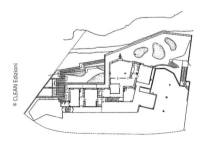

© CLEAN Edizioni

architects
Davide Pacanowski

type
residential

construction
1955

41. Villa Oro

Via Orazio 27
80122, Naples

external viewing only

**Funicolare
di Mergellina** >
Sant'Antonio

This house, named after, Dr. Augusto Oro, who commissioned the construction, occupies an elongated site on the slopes of the Posillipo Hillside.

It is composed of a clever arrangement of blocks that harmonise perfectly with the landscape. The base structure in tuff stone seems to be part of the hillside from which it emerges, in contrast with the white-plastered, geometrical shapes of the upper elements that were obviously influenced by advanced international trends. The various structural blocks intersect with one another, in staggered, recessed and swivelled positions, creating open spaces for terraces and gardens. The house is designed to enjoy the panorama of the gulf of Naples, with windows facing the sea. The impact is increased by the narrow window frames and slender balustrades.

The living room floor features a famous majolica tile scene of the gulf of Naples by the architects, Cosenza and Rudofsky, who also designed much of the interior and furnishings. The division of the property into different apartments has altered the layout, although the interesting façades can still be admired from the sea or from the street of Largo Sermoneta below.

© CLEAN Edizioni

© Giuliana Vespere

architects
Luigi Cosenza,
Bernard Rudofsky

type
residential

construction
1937

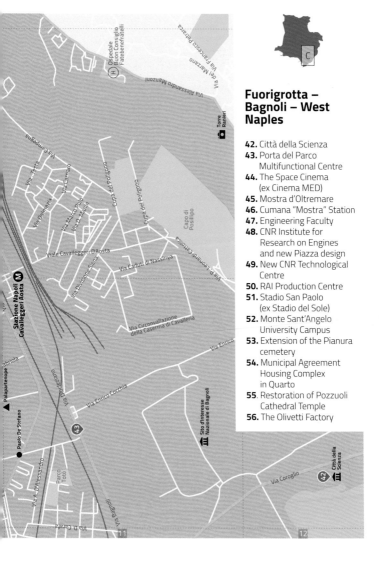

Fuorigrotta – Bagnoli – West Naples

42. Città della Scienza

Via Coroglio 57 and 104
80124, Naples

Tue - Sun / 10 am - 4 pm
Mon / closed

+39 081 7352220
contact@cittadellascienza.it
www.cittadellascienza.it

 Cumana > Bagnoli

This complex multiple project was constructed in three stages.

In 2001 the Museo Vivo della Scienza was inaugurated in a 19th century decommissioned factory on the seafront, (later destroyed by fire in 2013). The solid continuity of the various enclosed building façades formed a contrast with the dynamic layout of the terrain with continuous routes encircling the complex.

The new structure built in 2003, was constructed based on the form of the previous building to emphasise the integration between the surrounding urban space and the buildings on the site that include an Events Space, a Business Innovation Centre, offices, and a training and development space in a vast central area.

The Corporea – Human Body Museum was opened to the public in 2017, housed in a trapezoidal structure where a series of panoramic terraces filter the landscape through vertical gardens. The west side has a fascinating sinuous façade shaded by continuous terracotta *brise-soleil* screening. The large domed building houses the Planetarium.

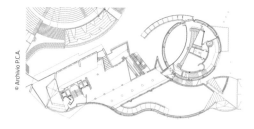

© Archivio P.C.A.

© Fabio Donato

architects
Pica Ciamarra Associati

type
museum

construction
2001 / 2003 / 2017

43. Porta del Parco Multifunctional Centre

Via Diocleziano 341
80124, Naples

external viewing only

www.comune.napoli.it

2 > Cavalleggeri d'Aosta

Cumana > Agnano

An ambitious industrial transformation plan is under way on the site of the ex-Ilva steelworks at Bagnoli. It has experienced dozens of operational difficulties, which involve the development of a new part of the city and new integrated tourist services. One of the completed interventions is the Porta del Parco, designed as the access to a large fully equipped public park.

The architect, Silvio d'Ascia, designed it as a vast public space open on several levels without continuity between interior and exterior. A monolithic slab distributes the access flow towards the various activities positioned on different levels; large sloped surfaces compensate the gradual difference in height, over eight metres, between the city level (Via Nuova Bagnoli) and the height of the future urban park.

This complex forms a hub of integrated services covering a total of over 40,000 square metres, with about 16,500 square metres of semi-underground parking. It is a functional blend of different activities, focussed on well-being, culture, and leisure time. Unfortunately, although the building was completed in time, it has not yet been opened to the public because of perennial bureaucratic problems.

© Silvio d'Ascia Architecture

© Barbara Jodice

architects
Silvio d'Ascia, MWH

type
multi-purpose building

construction
2013

44. The Space Cinema (ex Cinema MED)

Viale Giochi del Mediterraneo 36
80125, Naples

open to the public

www.thespacecinema.it

 2 > Cavalleggeri d'Aosta

 Cumana > Agnano

The regular geometrical structure of this multiplex movie theatre covers a 300×45 metre plot, the long side built along Viale Giochi del Mediterraneo. The area is divided by a green planted zone separating two buildings, one for a two storey car park, and the other, a structure composed of 11 movie theatres.

A projecting roof covers the entrance "piazza", and movie-goers enter through the full height glass façade into the large foyer that directs them towards stairs and elevators and the various movie theatres separated by glass partitions.

The interiors are clad with sound absorbent MDF panels with wood facing. On the lengthwise sides of the theatre regular shafts of light from the exterior provide lighting. The external cladding is composed of ventilated, blind curtain walls for the stairways, while the office spaces feature horizontal window openings. The minimal garden project, designed by the agronomist, Fabrizio Cembalo Sambiase, includes walkways, flower beds and water features, taking advantage of the sloping terrain, echoing the concept of the narrow terraced vineyards of the adjacent Phlegrean hills.

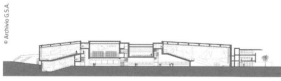

© Archivio G.S.A.

© Vittorio Guida

architects
Giancarlo Scognamiglio,
Antonio Costa

type
cinema

construction
2003

45. Mostra d'Oltremare

**Piazzale Vincenzo Tecchio,
Viale John Fitzgerald Kennedy,
Via Terracina**
80125, Naples

open to the public

+39 081 7258000
info@mostradoltremare.it
www.mostradoltremare.it

 2 > Campi Flegrei

 Cumana > Mostra

The *Triennial Exhibition of Overseas Italian Territories* covers a surface of over a million square metres, and was completed in record time under the direction of the Government Commissioner, Vincenzo Tecchio.

This intervention, part of the Fuorigrotta redevelopment plan, addressed several needs in a single project: firstly it answered the desire of the Fascist regime to celebrate the glory of the empire, and secondly, it contributed to the expansion of the city towards the west, according to the Town Planning Scheme under way, and finally, it provided an opportunity for young architects to take part in an amazing professional experience.

The planimetric and volumetric plan, composed of a right-angled grid system with two main axes, one in a longitudinal direction and the other transversal, site of the Esedra fountain, was designed by Marcello Canino, while the green areas within the entire park were the work of Luigi Piccinato and Carlo Cocchia.

This matrix contains the 36 buildings within the Mostra d'Oltremare site, rather like a collection of examples of modern outdoor architecture of great urban and architectural merit. Of particular interest are the ex-office building designed by Marcello Canino, with the rear reconstruction in 1952 by Delia Maione and restoration by Luigi Casalini; the Tower of Nations by Venturino Ventura, whose

© CLEAN Edizioni

architects	type	construction
various	exhibition hall	1940 / 1952

Piazzale Vincenzo Tecchio,
Viale John Fitzgerald Kennedy,
Via Terracina
80125, Naples

open to the public

+39 081 7258000
info@mostradoltremare.it
www.mostradoltremare.it

 2 > Campi Flegrei

 Cumana > Mostra

restoration, not yet completed, was designed by Corvino + Multari; the Mediterranean Theatre by Nino Barillà, Vincenzo Gentile, Filippo Mellia and Giuseppe Sambito, with interior design by Luigi Piccinato was recently restored by Cherubino Gambardella; the restaurant and swimming pool by Carlo Cocchia, whose façade fresco was executed by Enrico Prampolini, was restored by Pica Ciamarra Associati; the Latin American Pavilion was designed by Bruno La Padula, originally composed of three structures around a garden courtyard, but which, after bombing during the war, was rebuilt in its current design based on the project in 1952 by Michele Capobianco, Arrigo Marsiglia and Alfredo Sbriziol. It was partly rebuilt in 2000 by the Gambardella firm; the Arena Flegrea by Giulio De Luca, was demolished and rebuilt with improved acoustics; the large Golden Cube building, covered in mosaics by Mario Zanetti, Luigi Racheli and Paolo Zella Melillo, was restored by the Gambardella firm (see photo and drawing); the Cabrini Church, ex-Pavilion of the African Christian Rite by Roberto Pane, proposes certain archetypal elements of the classic basilica design in an unusual manner; the Rhodes Pavilion by Giovan Battista Ceas, is completely clad in Taranto stone.

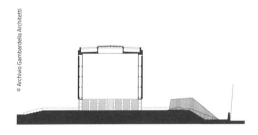

© Archivio Gambardella Architetti

46. Cumana "Mostra" Station

Piazzale Vincenzo Tecchio
80125, Naples

open to the public

 2 > Campi Flegrei

 Cumana > Mostra

Opened at the same time as the new *Triennial Exhibition of Overseas Italian Territories*, the Cumana railway station, designed by Frediano Frediani, combines the same successful blend of classical architecture and modern style as his design of the Via Leopardi station.

The architect opted for a circular layout, appropriate to the position of the station in the centre of the large empty space close to the main entrance to the Mostra d'Oltremare. The design recalls round Greek and Roman temples, emphasised by the slender columns around the perimeter on the side near the Mostra d'Oltremare entrance.

The station is composed of two cylinders of different heights: the central area is taller than the peripheral section, enabling the interior to capture direct light through a series of narrow rectangular openings set in the upper part of the perimeter, as well as through the glass brick roof supported by radial beams branching out from the single pillar in the geometrical centre of the atrium and entire composition.

The station underwent restoration performed by Nicola Pagliara, and completed in 1990.

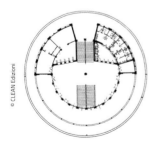

© CLEAN Edizioni

© Giuliana Vespere

architects
Frediano Frediani

type
station

construction
1940

47. Engineering Faculty

Piazzale Vincenzo Tecchio 80
80125, Naples

open to the public

contactcenter@unina.it
www.unina.it

 2 > Campi Flegrei

Cumana > Mostra

Like other university faculties after the Second World War, the new Engineering Faculty, required greater space outside the historic city centre for lecture halls and scientific laboratories. It was built in Piazzale Tecchio, close to the main entrance of the Mostra d'Oltremare trade centre and where the new football stadium was under construction.

The core elements of the project are the main structure in Viale Augusto, designed along similar lines to the social housing apartment blocks built for the homeless (1949), and connected by a portico and a cloister that form the access to the lecture halls and other service areas.

The main façade forms a theatrical setting overlooking the vast square and is composed of 11 floors, divided into a regular glass and clinker grid system, set on a projecting base structure faced with a large mosaic work by Paolo Ricci in different shades of blue.

The portico atrium leads to the taller building, with a large space open onto a courtyard garden. The auditorium, administration offices and the large lecture halls are located on the first floor, accessed by open metal stairways, in typical traditional Neapolitan style.

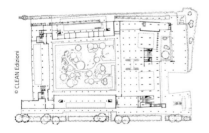

© CLEAN Edizioni

© Giuliana Vespere

architects
Luigi Cosenza

type
university

construction
1965 / 1980

48. CNR Institute for Research on Engines and new Piazza design

Via Guglielmo Marconi 4 / Piazzale Vincenzo Tecchio
80125, Naples

partly open to the public

+39 081 7177111
direttore@im.cnr.it
www.im.cnr.it

 2 > Campi Flegrei

 Cumana > Mostra

This project was the result of a competition held in 1984 to replace the old building designed by Camillo Guerra in 1939, and is part of a wider program for the construction of a technological hub.

The building features a clean pure design with aluminium façades in contrast with the solid base. The main focus was to create a close relationship with the environment, using technological solutions such as rainwater recovery and recycling.

The new building inspired the design for the urban transformation of the area in front of the institute. The pedestrian area is paved with wood crossed by water trickling from a large graduated fountain, and bordered by 40-metre obelisks that recall 18th century traditional Neapolitan "macchine da festa": the Time and Fluids Tower, in wood, with wind-activated sound machines and a screen-sail for laser rays, the Memory Tower, in iron and stone, like a periscope focussing on the sea and the old city, and the Information Tower in aluminium, that traces the evolution of information systems.

© Archivio P.C.A.

architects
CNR Institute for Research
on Engines: Pica Ciamarra
Associati, Giuseppe Squillante
Square: Pica Ciamarra
Associati

type
public space, offices

construction
CNR Institute for Research
on Engines: 1989
Square: 1990

49. New CNR Technological Centre

Via Guglielmo Marconi 4
80125, Naples

partly open to the public

+39 081 7682245
irc@irc.cnr.it
www.irc.cnr.it

 2 > Campi Flegrei

 Cumana > Mostra

This new complex integrates the CNR Technological Research Centre, housing the Combustion Research Institute and the Institute for Environmental Electromagnetic Survey. The complex is composed of three blocks, each three storeys high, in a U-shape layout, creating an internal courtyard which separates each structure and provides natural light inside the buildings. Although these are considered as three distinct institutes, the buildings are connected by internal passages to facilitate circulation. The two parallel structures are destined for specific research work while the transversal block houses technical office spaces and coordination centres.

The external façades are clad completely in terracotta with a surface striated in different directions to create plays of shade and an unusual texture that changes according to variations in sunlight.

Energy saving has been a major focus in this design. Sensors are used to detect human presence in each space, to trigger lighting and heating according to necessity, preventing waste. The latest anti-seismic technology has been incorporated in the base of each building.

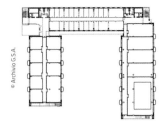

© Archivio G.S.A.

architects	**type**	**construction**
Giancarlo Scognamiglio	offices	2017

50. RAI Production Centre

Via Guglielmo Marconi 9
80125, Naples

open to the public only
during specific events

+39 081 7251111

www.rai.it

 2 > Campi Flegrei

 Cumana > Mostra

The centre forms a small television city composed of 5 buildings on a 4.5 acre site located between the Mostra d'Oltremare and the CNR centre. The Rai buildings are connected by overhead projecting glass roofing. The façade overlooking the street includes a services building and a linear structure housing the offices and auditorium. The TV and radio production studios are located at the rear in the direction of the Mostra d'Oltremare.

The most striking element is the massive tiered auditorium projecting over the street, sustained by six supporting elements that taper towards the base, creating a dramatic entrance.

The auditorium remained in disuse for years until 2004, when Gnosis progetti and Alessandro Castagnaro, with Renato Sparacio (structural engineering), and Enrico Lanzillo (technical installations), undertook the restoration of the auditorium's infrastructures and technical systems. The project was aimed at recovering and enhancing the architectural style and restoring the original volumes which had been altered several times over the years. The project included upgrading the acoustics of the auditorium.

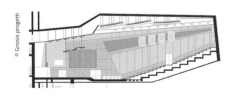

© Gnosis progetti

architects
Mario De Renzi, Renato
Avolio De Martino, Raffaele
Contigiani / Gnosis progetti,
Alessandro Castagnaro

type
theatre, offices

construction
1963 / 2007

51. Stadio San Paolo (ex Stadio del Sole)

Piazzale Vincenzo Tecchio
80125, Naples

open to the public only
during specific events

 2 > Campi Flegrei

 Cumana > Mostra

Initially destined for the eastern side of Naples, the new municipal sports stadium was designed by Carlo Cocchia and a talented team of architects and engineers, winners of a contest held just after the Second World War. After years of discussion, it was finally constructed in the west of Naples, at Fuorigrotta, near the Mostra d'Oltremare trade centre, and was opened in the late 1950s.

The stadium is outstanding for its elegant structural design and light airy effect thanks to the slender framework and staircases positioned at regular intervals, that almost seem suspended. In the original design, the second level seemed to almost float in the air, but the heavy roof, added for the World Football Championship in 1990 had an oppressive impact on the structure, eliminating the play of light and shadow and radically distorting the former perception. The stadium is currently undergoing technical and structural upgrading to bring it to the standards required by modern public structures.

© Archivio Comune di Napoli

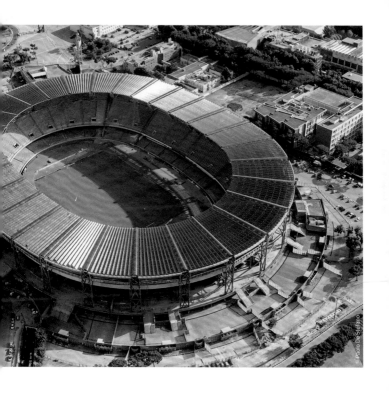

architects	type	construction
Carlo Cocchia	stadium	1959

52. Monte Sant'Angelo University Campus

Strada vicinale Cupa Cintia 21
80126, Naples

open to the public

contactcenter@unina.it
www.unina.it

**R6 / C33 / 180
/ 614** > Cintia-Monte
Sant'Angelo

The final project for new University campus, located in a hilly area overlooking the Fuorigrotta and Soccavo neighbourhoods, was signed by Michele Capobianco and Massimo Pica Ciamarra. The aim of the project was to relieve the congestion of the University facilities in the city centre by creating new modern and more ample structures.

Capobianco, with Infrasud progetti and Daniele Zagaria, then developed the project for the buildings of the Faculty of Economics and Commerce, and for the "consolidated" classrooms and the common areas finished in 1993, while the classrooms of the Faculty of Engineering and the Faculty of Physics and Mathematics are still under construction.

Capobianco's stereometric decomposed design, based on cube root and the use of colour, is not simply decorative but typical of his architectural expression, strongly influenced by Swedish design.

The lecture halls and internal spaces are arranged along gallery walkways, sometimes lit by overhead skylights, and the dynamic perception of space results from the alternating surfaces in raw concrete with an abstract texture and the use of vibrant colour even used to paint internal systems piping.

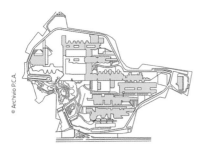

© Archivio P.C.A.

© Salvatore Giordano

architects
Michele Capobianco,
Massimo Pica Ciamarra

type
university

construction
1993 / in progress

53. Extension of the Pianura cemetery

Strada comunale Cimitero 86
80126, Naples

Mon - Sun / 7.30 am - 6 pm

+39 081 7956367

www.comune.napoli.it

Circumflegrea >
Pianura

This intervention was carried out by Inter-progetti (structural work) and CDS ingegne-ria (technical systems), and is part of a larger project by the Nea'Cropolis company, charged with other Neapolitan developments includ-ing the extension of the Soccavo and Barra cemeteries.

The project will extend the existing 19th cen-tury cemetery layout, with burial grounds, monuments, a garden, two service buildings, a columbarium with an internal courtyard, and an open courtyard flanked by two further columbarium buildings, one of which was al-ready built by the Municipality in the 1990s.

The plan includes burial grounds, service buildings, and new columbarium with funer-ary niches and crypts, that will extend, in a form similar to the existing building, an L-shaped, four-storey construction plus hypo-geum. The building has light transparent fa-çades, composed of voids and solid elements, in contrast with the stereometric severity of the existing building. The diamond patterned metal gridwork in various sizes and colours provides an intense play of light, as well as adequate ventilation for the space.

© Paolo De Stefano

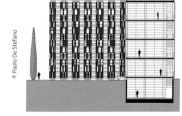

architects
Tstudio – Guendalina Salimei,
Paolo De Stefano

type
cemetery

construction
2018

54. Municipal Agreement Housing Complex in Quarto

Via Crocillo
80010, Quarto (Na)

external viewing only

Circumflegrea >
Quarto centro

The design of this complex is based on three rectangular blocks set in two C-shaped constructions facing each other along the main north-south road, and forming a central courtyard. The external façades are clad with a continuous exposed brick surface, interrupted only by staircases and balconies, set at a 45 degree angle, which shed sharp shadows on the brick walls. The façades surrounding the internal courtyard have an excellent rational design with clean pure lines. They feature a diaphragm of louvre shutters that slide to close the loggia terraces of each apartment. A unifying element of the entire complex is the plinth base in lava stone, to recall the Campi Flegrei volcanic eruptions.

The external layout also provides for private vegetable plots, a nod to the agricultural traditions of the area. Each building is equipped with passive solar energy systems composed of integrated solar chimneys, and active solar panel energy. Each apartment has a personal solar collector surface for its daily domestic hot water supply.

© Studio F64 – Cappelli & Crisciuolo

architects
Corvino + Multari

type
residential

construction
2014

55. Restoration of Pozzuoli Cathedral Temple

Via Duomo, Rione Terra
80078, Pozzuoli (Na)

Sat / 10 am - 12 pm,
5.30 pm - 7.30 pm
Sun / 10 am - 1 pm,
5.30 pm - 7.30 pm
Mon - Fri / closed

+39 388 1019712
info@associazionenemea.it
www.cattedralepozzuoli.it

 Cumana > Pozzuoli

This Temple was a refined example of Roman architecture from the Augustan age, later transformed into a church in the early 6th century, and restored in 1647 to a design by Bartolomeo Picchiatti and Cosimo Fanzago. The recent restoration project, winner of an international contest, was drawn up by a coordinated team of experts in different fields, to provide solutions for the complex problems caused by the extremely unusual site. The intervention combined conservation intervention as well as contemporary architecture, to respect the existing Baroque style and remaining archaeological elements: this was aimed at ensuring the transference of the entire palimpsest for future use, both archaeological and cultural. The team focused on the exceptionally evocative impact of the accumulated historic stratification and the complex vestiges present in the Cathedral Temple, using airy transparent devices to recall the destroyed elements, and allude to the strongly theatrical effect of the former Baroque decoration.

In 2003, the Gnosis firm completed the restoration and construction of the underground archaeological route of some of the Roman insulae in the Rione Terra area.

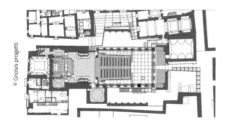

© Gnosis progetti

© Gnosis progetti

architects
Marco Dezzi Bardeschi, Gnosis progetti, Renato De Fusco, Alessandro Castagnaro

type
church, museum

construction
2014

56. The Olivetti Factory

Via Campi Flegrei 34
80078, Pozzuoli (Na)

external viewing only

 M1B > 5020

This complex has a cruciform layout designed to respect the technical and functional needs of the factory while adapting it to the natural slope of the site. The design provides maximum façade orientation, and at the same time, excellent distribution of open spaces combined with enclosed areas. The building is perfectly integrated in the landscape.

The various services such as a medical facility, library, and canteen, plus the beautiful landscaping designed by Pietro Porcinai, clearly indicate the Olivetti vision in aiming to provide maximum welfare for his workers, combining the needs of an industrial company and the community values of traditional society.

Among the most successful features of the project are the sloping roof on the main building that provides maximum light inside the workspace, and the rainwater drainage system, hidden inside hollow pillars, so that no drainpipes are visible on the façades.

The structure was not modified to any great extent by the extensions added later in 1970, and designed by Roberto Guiducci and the Tekne company, with the consulting expertise of the original architect, Luigi Cosenza.

architects
Luigi Cosenza

type
offices

construction
1954 / 1970

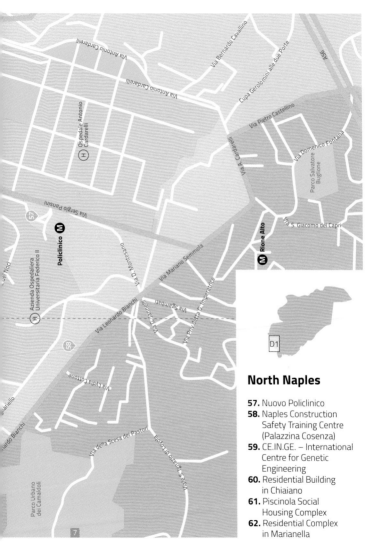

North Naples

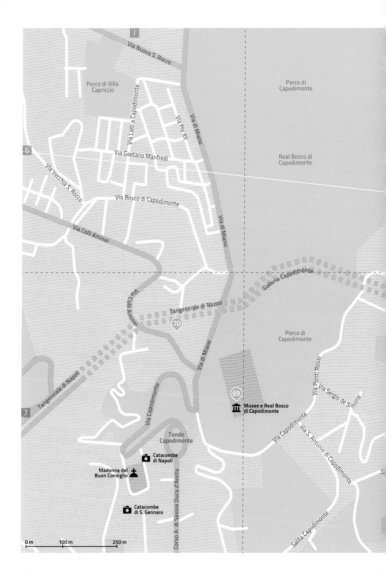

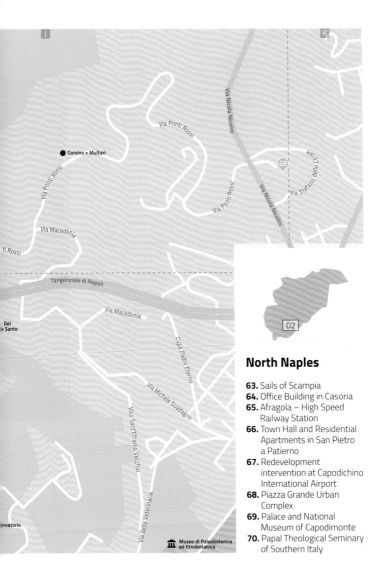

Corvino • Multari

North Naples

57. Nuovo Policlinico

Via Sergio Pansini 5
80131, Naples

open to the public

+39 081 7463766
diraup@unina.it
www.policlinico.unina.it

 1 > Policlinico

This university hospital complex was built in the 1960s adjacent to the Cardarelli Hospital built thirty years earlier, to expand the hospital facilities in the area. It is composed of numerous buildings spread over a vast area connected by long avenues at ground level and by underground circuits. The complex is made up of 18 buildings for the university clinics, several low structures for research activities, university lectures and administration, and other specific buildings like the biological tower, anatomy institutes, and the auditorium.

The tall slender hospital buildings are based on a standard sanatorium layout, with patients' rooms facing south west, and the corridors on the opposite sides. The façades are divided by horizontal bands of windows of various heights, specifically designed to give patients external views whether standing, seated, or lying in bed.

The excessive distance between the different buildings, and the mediocre finishes contributed to the partial failure of this project, although, in itself, the complex is commendable for its excellent functional layout.

©Pablo De Stefano

architects
Carlo Cocchia, Cesare Blasi,
Mario Boudet, Fabrizio
Cocchia, Onorina Frazzi,
Massimo Nunziata,
Gabriella Padovano,
Michele Pizzolorusso

type
hospital

construction
1971

58. Naples Construction Safety Training Centre (Palazzina Cosenza)

Via Leonardo Bianchi 36
80131, Naples

partly open to the public

+39 081 7705749
info@cfsnapoli.it
www.cfsnapoli.it

 1 > Policlinico

This reinforced concrete building, designed by Luigi Cosenza in the 1950s, features an upper floor that projects out over the glass fronted ground floor, overlooking the street. The original design was altered considerably in later years. The building was planned as the first block of a larger complex forming a large training centre for the building industry. The original plan was inspired by the Olivetti Factory at Pozzuoli, designed at the same time by the same architect, Cosenza.

The recovery project by studio Od'A to provide a new function for the building, includes a series of operations to restore the original design, recovering the most important elements, eliminating any superfluous additions and cladding, as well as the completion of the end wall on the eastern side. This modern restoration has revealed the original architectural style and facings that distinguished this building, including the ceramic mosaic finish on the circular pillars, and the upper floors that taper towards the exterior. The solid and void areas of the façades have been restored, as well as the first floor flower planters, and the tuff stone embankment wall.

© Archivio Od'A

© Fabio Florena

architects
Luigi Cosenza / Od'A officina
d'architettura

type
offices

construction
1955 / 2012

59. CE.IN.GE. – International Centre for Genetic Engineering

Via Gaetano Salvatore 486
80131, Naples

partly open to the public

+39 081 3737937

www.ceinge.unina.it

 1 > Policlinico

The CE.IN.GE., located at the edge of the University of Naples Medicine and Surgery Faculty, is a centre for genetic engineering and biotechnology. It houses offices, laboratories, lecture and seminar halls, libraries, and a conference hall.

The initial intervention, designed in 1992 and completed in 2004, was the three storey central structure, designed for further extension with an additional floor. The technical systems are housed on the roof, enclosed in a metal structure, an identifying element on the skyline.

The 2007 project, completed in various stages, included the addition of a fourth floor on the centre block and a new building constructed in the gap between the street level and the base of the central building. It contains a two-storey car park, and a third floor for study rooms, laboratories, classrooms, and lecture halls. The upper open space will house a dynamic future conference hall.

© Archivio P.C.A.

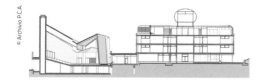

© Archivio P.C.A.

architects
Pica Ciamarra Associati,
Carmine Colucci,
Renato Carrelli

type
offices

construction
1992 / in progress (extension)

60. Residential Building in Chiaiano

Traversa Giovanni Antonio Campano 10
80145, Naples

external viewing only

 1 > Chiaiano

This new residential complex, built around an enclosed courtyard, replaces a former construction. It has five floors, one of which is underground and destined for an auto repair garage. Each of the two staircases lead to three apartments of various sizes (from 48 to 73 square metres) with a total of six apartments per floor, all with loggias or balconies. Both façades, on the street side and overlooking the internal courtyard, have windows. On the ground floor, as well as some apartments, there are also two spaces for offices or retail stores, while the roof includes six private terraces that belong to the apartments on the floor below.

The façades feature different elements: larger balconies on the south-west corner, but smaller on the front external sides, while the internal courtyard façades have windows of various sizes. Traditional materials were used for the finishes: pre-painted aluminium for external window frames, and metal balustrades, for better integration with the surrounding neighbourhood. The external façades have a coloured plaster finish, and the plinth base is clad with light grey ceramic slabs.

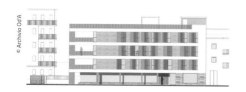

© Archivio OdA

© Archivio OdA

architects
Od'A officina d'architettura

type
residential

construction
2012

61. Piscinola Social Housing Complex

Via Giovanni Antonio Campano
80145, Naples

external viewing only

 1 > Chiaiano

This complex was the result of a competition launched in 2003 by the Naples Municipality to replace a prefabricated building that housed 126 families left homeless after the 1980 earthquake. The winning Neapolitan firm, Gambardella Architetti, designed a series of buildings arranged in a C-shaped formation around a courtyard aimed at providing a place for the community to meet and socialise, in an area of the city where this was lacking. The scope was to construct the new buildings around the existing prefabricated structure, so that once the new housing was completed, the families could be transferred to their new homes, and the old prefabricated building would be destroyed. This would leave an open public space and room for underground parking. However, the old building is still partially occupied and it has not been possible to complete the new apartments. The internal courtyard façades are clad with intense cobalt blue tiles, while the external façades are mainly finished in white plaster with blue inserts.

All internal and external façades have numerous openings, balconies, and loggias, deliberately left free to allow inhabitants to personalise the spaces to their own taste.

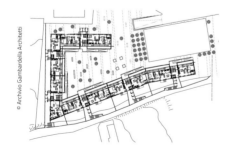

© Archivio Gambardella Architetti

architects
Gambardella Architetti

type
residential

construction
2012

62. Residential Complex in Marianella

Via della Bontà, Via Salvatore Battaglia, Via Marianella
80145, Naples

external viewing only

 1 > Chiaiano

This irregular plot was divided into a chequerboard layout with an alternating modular series of courtyards and apartment buildings. The two main courtyard façades feature slender steel loggias, while in the centre of each of the four smaller courtyards is a staircase tower structure that provides access to the surrounding apartment buildings. The structure has an openwork façade clad in glass prisms.

Around the perimeter, following that of the pre-existent courtyards, is a yellow tuff stone wall that creates a link between modern and traditional aspects, as well as a connection between the new apartment buildings and the old rural houses of Marianella, nearby.

Each apartment, 65 square metres in size, has a view over one of the small access courtyards, one of the two grand courtyards or the public roadway.

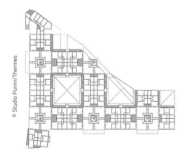

© Studio Purini/Thermes

© Studio Purini/Thermes

architects
Studio Purini/Thermes,
Aldo Aymonino, Gianfranco
Neri, Nicole Surchat

type
residential

construction
1988

63. Sails of Scampia

Via Antonio Labriola,
Viale della Resistenza,
Via Tancredi Galimberti
80145, Naples

external viewing only

 1 > Piscinola

The uncertain outcome of this complex project has marked the history of this series of low cost, social housing buildings designed by Franz Di Salvo, inspired by the *Cité radieuse* by Le Corbusier.

The "tent style" concept, is composed of two parallel stair-like structures, separated by a narrow void containing suspended walkways and staircases to corridors on each apartment building floor. They also provide socialising space for the inhabitants.

Today, Di Salvo's vast architectural dream is considered a failure, probably because of the lack of services that were never constructed, and because of the difficult social condition of the inhabitants.

Today, only 4 of the 7 original "sails" still exist, since 3 were demolished between 1997 and 2003, however, redevelopment plans for the area are under way as the Municipality has decided to demolish other 3 buildings and restore one single "sail" in homage to this fine example of architecture; it will be later transformed to house public office spaces.

architects
Francesco Di Salvo

type
residential

construction
1975

64. Office Building in Casoria

**Via Francesco Orefice,
Via Pietro Nenni**
80026, Casoria (Na)

external viewing only

+39 081 7580509
info@griecam.com
www.griecam.com

 C1N > 1514

This project is part of an area undergoing industrial expansion, characterised by the lack of previous buildings, and on the boundary of the consolidated urban fabric. The intervention involved the transformation of an uncompleted construction left in its raw condition, exposed to time and weather. It provided an opportunity for new design, aimed at creating a unified context and strengthening a sense of local identity.
The building is composed of three floors above ground for office space, and a basement level for parking and storage. The aim to restore the building, giving it a unified effect, was achieved through the use of a *brise-soleil* system composed of curved extruded aluminium slats with increased spacing for a lighter effect towards the top of the building. Natural light penetrates the building directly from the south side, and indirectly through a light well provided by the glass elevator shaft. The shaft crosses the entire building down to the basement level, and diffuses the overhead light captured from the glass opening in the staircase tower.

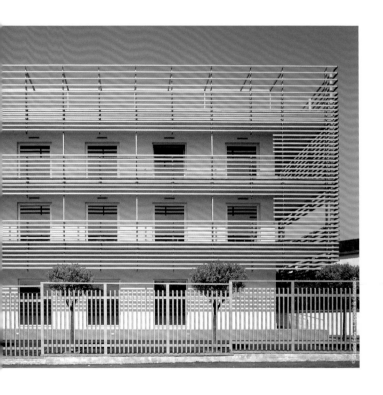

architects	type	construction
Corvino + Multari	offices	2010

65. Afragola – High Speed Railway Station

Via Arena
80021, Afragola (Na)

open to the public

www.fsitaliane.it

Frecciarossa >
Napoli Afragola

Located 12 km north of Naples, when this station will be fully functional, it will become the access gateway to the city. Zaha Hadid took a piece of anonymous, neglected countryside and transformed it with her masterpiece, like a cathedral in the desert almost seeming to announce a return to the ancient Campania felix. A spectacular, futuristic sculpture that shows the democratic face of an architecture celebrated by the international star system. The compositional principle of this dynamic, fluid structure, designed like a bridge-building suspended over the rail system, was inspired by the passenger flow and speed of the trains that transit through this station. The image that inspired the architect was that of "a river that has carved its bed in solid rock. The atrium flows through the centre under the fluid glass roofing. Both sides of the canyon are eroded by traffic flow".

The entrances are located at each end of the complex and lead passengers to the atrium in the centre of the bridge, where the waiting rooms, ticket offices, and several stores are located. The sinuous concrete, steel and glass structure also houses a shopping mall.

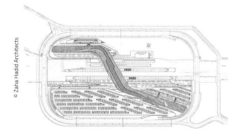

© Zaha Hadid Architects

© Photograph by Hufton+Crow

architects	type	construction
Zaha Hadid Architects	station	2017

66. Town Hall and Residential Apartments in San Pietro a Patierno

Piazza Giovanni Guarino
80144, Naples

partly open to the public

+39 081 7952018

www.comune.napoli.it

This refined project designed by Francesco Venezia was part of a far wider redevelopment scheme in the centre of the old quarter of San Pietro a Patierno, connected to the Naples Municipality since 1926, and today, a city suburb close to the Capodichino Airport. The project involved the reorganisation of the main piazza in San Pietro, with a necessary, although restrained, monumental identity, in harmony with the 18th century Church of San Pietro in the piazza. The project included the construction of a new municipal building for administration offices, a military barracks, and residential apartments. The new curved structure is cleverly linked with the surrounding historical context thanks to careful urban planning. The construction has a plain modern design, and the two main façades feature a series of quadrangular windows of different sizes.

 **C87 / 182** > San Pietro a Patierno

© CLEAN Edizioni

architects
Francesco Venezia

type
residential, offices

construction
1999

67. Redevelopment intervention at Capodichino International Airport

Viale Fulco Ruffo di Calabria
80144, Naples

open to the public

+39 081 7896259

www.aeroportodinapoli.it

Alibus > Aeroporto di Capodichino

The interventions by the Gnosis architectural firm at the Naples airport in recent years were focussed on reorganising the arrivals area, the non-Schengen departure areas, check-in and boarding gate areas, the construction of retail stores and new rest room facilities, plus new signage throughout. The unified design established a central theme, creating a style that represents a type of brand identity within the airport, achieved by using signs, shapes and materials that, while remaining specific to their purpose, echo each other throughout.

The inspiration for the various projects was the dynamic impression generated by flight. This influenced the sloping surfaces of the check-in and boarding gate desks and certain walls, and the use of glass for transparent and reflective effects. With a view to constant evolution in airport buildings that demand frequent changes and upgrades to cope with the needs of passengers and operators, all interventions are designed to be flexible and reversible, while maintaining the quality and durability of construction and finishing materials, cleverly integrating innovation and local traditional craftsmanship.

© Gnosis progetti

architects
Gnosis progetti

type
airport

construction
2015

68. Piazza Grande Urban Complex

Via Nicola Nicolini
80141, Naples

external viewing only

Clearly visible from the viaduct on the ring road highway around the city, Piazza Grande is one of the largest interventions that has been developed in Naples for decades. It is located in the so-called "Red bridge" district, named after the remains of a Roman arched brick aqueduct only a few metres from the entrance to the complex designed by Aldo Loris Rossi to replace a former industrial building. The complex is composed of 200 residential apartments and integrated services, including a school, shops and leisure facilities.

The large complex, composed of curved and cylindrical forms, is inspired by the architecture of Lloyd Wright and the Royal Cresent and Circus in Bath, as are many of the buildings by this architect, and seems to be completely independent of its surroundings. The main lower structure, surrounded by six towers, 36 metres high, is circular in shape and encloses a vast space about 100 metres in diameter that incorporates green park areas, sports facilities and underground garages.

🚌 **254 / C63** > Nicolini

© CLEAN Edizioni

Tiziana Vespere

architects
Aldo Loris Rossi, Annalisa
Pignalosa, Luigi Rivieccio

type
residential, retails, offices

construction
1989

69. Palace and National Museum of Capodimonte

Via Miano 2
80131, Naples

Thu - Tue / 8.30 am - 7.30 pm
Wen / closed

+39 081 7499111
mu-cap@beniculturali.it
www.museocapodimonte.
beniculturali.it

C63 > Museo
e Real Bosco
di Capodimonte

The construction of a palace on the Capodimonte Hills, was a decision by Charles VII of Naples and Sicily, to house the magnificent art collection left by his mother, Elisabetta Farnese. The construction lasted for most of the 18th century and was completed only in 1838. After 1816, under the rule of Ferdinand Bourbon of Two Sicilies, it was converted to a royal residence, and was later donated to the Italian State in 1920. Following extensive restoration work, in 1957, the palace was dedicated specifically to house the Farnese Collection for which it had been originally designed.

The palace has two floors plus a third under the eaves, and a large balcony around the roof cornice. It has a rectangular layout with three courtyards and two wings that extend at each end. The façade is Neoclassical style with grey piperno stone pilasters in contrast with the red plaster finish.

The famous enormous park that surrounds the palace was designed by Ferdinando Sanfelice in 1743 and is planted with centuries old trees. An English garden was designed by Friedrich Dehnhardte in the 19th century.

architects
Antonio Medrano, Antonio
Canevari / Ezio Bruno
De Felice, Ennio Amodio

type
museum

construction
1765 / 1957

70. Papal Theological Seminary of Southern Italy

Viale Colli Aminei 2
80131, Naples

open to the public

+39 081 7413343
segreteria.preside@pftim.it
www.pftim.it

This complex, set in lush green surroundings, is located on the Capodimonte hill, not far from the palace. It is built on the site of a former 18th century villa.

The different buildings of the complex are positioned on the site around a centuries old magnolia. The fair faced concrete façades feature concrete brise soleil elements that create an interesting composition. The university complex is composed of two distinct centres: the first, and main structure, houses the auditorium that seats 500 students. It has a triangular layout and also contains a library and a chapel, while the second building houses the lecture halls and administration offices. The triangular auditorium forms the core of the complex and is flooded with natural light that pours through the steeply sloping roof with its spire effect that provides a new landmark, visible from several points around the city.

 604 > Colli Aminei –
Ist. Teologia
Capodimonte

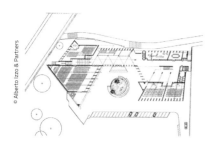

© Alberto Izzo & Partners

architects
Alberto Izzo & Partners

type
university

construction
1972

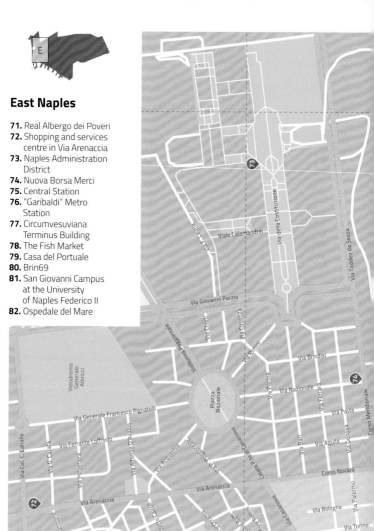

East Naples

Piazza
Giuseppe Garibaldi

76

Garibaldi Ⓜ

75 FS **Stazione**
Napoli Centrale

Via S. Spaventa

Via G. Ricciardi

Via Giuseppe Pica

Via San Cosmo Fuori Porta Nolana

77 FS **Circumvesuviana**

Corso Arnaldo Lucci

Via Galileo Ferraris

Via S. Brun

Via G. Manso

Via Padre Ludovico da Casoria

Via Padre Rocco

Via G. C. Capaccio

Via S. Maria d. Grazie a Loreto

Via M. Ciccone

Via G. Teppia

Via A. Toscano

Via Luigi Serio

Via Enrico Cosenz

Via Strettola S. Anna alle Paludi

Via C. Marino

Via Galileo Ferraris

Via Benedetto Brin

80

Via Benedetto Brin

Via A. Pacinotti

Via Alessandro Volta

Corso A. Lucci

Via B. Brin

Via Amerigo Vespucci

Via Ponte della Maddalena

78 FS

79

Calata Vittorio Veneto

Calata della Marinella

Molo Cesario Console

Corso Giuseppe Garibaldi

8

G

L

K

0 m   100 m   250 m

71. Real Albergo dei Poveri

Piazza Carlo III
80137, Naples

external viewing only

www.comune.napoli.it

 182 > Piazza Carlo III

In 1751, Ferdinando Fuga was commissioned by Charles II of the House of Bourbon to design this building to house the poor of the kingdom, calculated at about 8,000 in number. The work advanced slowly until 1819, when it was finally interrupted. Compared to the original project which was to include five courtyards running the whole length of the building for about 600 metres, the construction was limited to 400 metres with only three courtyards; nonetheless, the building did cover an impressive 103,000 square metres.

A monumental double staircase led to the main entrance and on into the central courtyard occupied by an X-shaped structure which was to have been a large church with a radial layout connected to the side wings through four transepts.

Today the building is in a bad state of disrepair despite the efforts of the current owners, the Naples Municipality, to maintain and preserve it with limited resources. For this reason, it is feared that the building may be decommissioned, although this has not been confirmed at present.

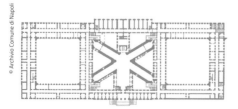

architects
Ferdinando Fuga

type
homeless shelter

construction
1751

72. Shopping and services centre in Via Arenaccia

Via Arenaccia 154
80141, Naples

open to the public

R5 > Arenaccia

This new shopping and services centre, opened in 2010, is based on the same shape and size as the former office building that occupied the site, designed in the 1960s by Franz Di Salvo, and later demolished because of its large asbestos content. The building has three floors plus two underground parking levels and has maintained the interesting raw concrete helical vehicle ramp that leads to roof level.

The new building, designed by Silvio d'Ascia with Tecnosystem, occupies almost a whole quadrangular site in the local neighbourhood grid system, and is composed of a compact parallelepiped clad in dark metal, interrupted by large windows with invisible frames. The glossy reflective surface and continuous window openings create a strong connection between interior and exterior, and the design of this new shopping centre has created a landmark in a neighbourhood characterised by conventional residential buildings.

© Silvio d'Ascia Architecture

© Barbara Iodice

architects
Silvio d'Ascia

type
retails, offices

construction
2010

73. Naples Administration District

**Via Nuova Poggioreale,
Via Taddeo da Sessa,
Corso Malta**
80143, Naples

partly open to the public

www.centrodirezionapoli.it

Circumvesuviana
> Napoli Centro
Direzionale

The master plan, that covers an area of over 270 acres, was designed by Kenzo Tange based on the original idea by Giulio De Luca, a few years previously; it was conceived to separate pedestrian and traffic circulation, laid out on different height levels. The skyscrapers and office buildings are built along a vast pedestrian concourse running east to west, with planted greenery and seating; the roadways, parking and service areas are organised on the lower level.

The architecture is standard international style, with imposing stereo-metric towers, built to monumental technological design using high tech materials and curtain walls whose mirrored surfaces reflect the architecture to infinity, plunging visitors into a metaphysical atmosphere. The global effect, in contrast with the Mediterranean character of the city, is reminiscent of Sant'Elia's "new city", in which striking buildings like the CNR towers rise, as if paying homage to the futuristic monumental skyscrapers, in almost Brutalist style, and to the geometrical design of the Hall of Justice with its three towers that soar above the horizontal step formation of the building's base.

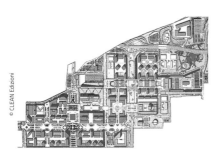

© CLEAN Edizioni

© Paolo De Stefano

architects
various

type
residential, retails, offices

construction
1990 - 1995

74. Nuova Borsa Merci

Corso Meridionale 58
80143, Naples

open to the public

+39 081 284193
info@assograneranapoli.com
www.assograneranapoli.com

1 / 2 > Garibaldi

Circumvesuviana >
Napoli Garibaldi

This project was the result of a national competition for the construction of a site for wholesale buying and selling of fresh fruit and vegetable produce. It was assigned to a team of designers composed of Michele Capobianco (leader), Riccardo Dalisi and Massimo Pica Ciamarra.
The building is located adjacent to the central railway station in an urban fabric based on the 19th century grid system. It is composed of a main block that seems suspended above a recessed ground floor glazed structure, set back from the street. Two strong lines of shadow created by the thick projecting roof slab and by the curved underside of the overhanging shelter formed by the first floor, emphasise the building's stereometric elegance. The interior has great impact: the full height entrance gallery is enhanced by a shaft of subtle light shed by the long skylight in the roof and defined by a series of walkways and ramps to create a dynamic and captivating space.

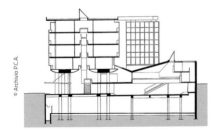

© Archivio P.C.A.

© Salvatore Giordano

architects
Michele Capobianco, Riccardo
Dalisi, Massimo Pica Ciamarra

type
offices

construction
1971

75. Central Station

Piazza Giuseppe Garibaldi
80142, Naples

open to the public

www.napolicentrale.it

 1 / 2 > Garibaldi

 Circumvesuviana >
Napoli Garibaldi

The station design was the result of a bid for tenders announced by the Italian Railways in 1954, aimed at replacing the historic, but outdated colonnaded structure by Nicola Breglia. The station was a combination of three projects which tied for the winning design, plus certain elements taken from a fourth project selected by the commission. The general layout and urban plan for the piazza were designed by the Cocchia team, while the organisation of the internal spaces was designed by the Battaglini team. The Nervi team was responsible for the roof design and the triangular framework of the entrance, sustained by unusual triple tapered supports designed by the group guided by Castiglioni. Alongside the extensive low covered area that houses the actual station is a 16 story office block.

The Italian Railways recently launched a restyling project for the station, which, together with the creation of a new subway station and the contextual urban redevelopment, has given new life to the piazza after years of neglect.

architects
Carlo Cocchia, Bruno Barinci,
Massimo Battaglini, Corrado
Cameli, Mario Campanella,
Giulio De Luca, Marino
Lombardi, Pier Luigi Nervi,
Luigi Piccinato, Giuseppe
Vaccaro, Ugo Viale, Bruno Zevi

type
station

construction
1966

76. "Garibaldi" Metro Station

Piazza Giuseppe Garibaldi
80142, Naples

open to the public

+39 800 639525
info@anm.it
www.anm.it

 1 / 2 > Garibaldi

 Circumvesuviana >
Napoli Garibaldi

The new metro station designed by Dominique Perrault is a complex hub that connects Metro Line 1 with the main railway station (in turn connected with Metro Line 2 and the Circumvesuviana Railway). It also gives access to shopping malls and provided the opportunity for redesigning the entire vast Piazza Garibaldi.

The design has great impact and features a huge overhead shelter composed of white tubular steel poles and large Teflon sails supported by eight layers of steel ribbing. It resembles a stylised forest, protecting the space underneath, set below street level. This level houses the shopping malls and ticket barriers, giving passengers access to a dramatic, close-knit network of escalators, seemingly suspended in space. Two works by Michelangelo Pistoletto are displayed on the final landing before the access to train platforms.

The piazza above has been redesigned with large pedestrian areas and a much more rational road system, following the years of chaos that defined this urban area for so long.

 © Dominique Perrault Architecture

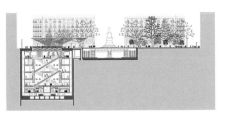

© Peppe Maisto / Dominique Perrault architecte / Adagp

architects
Dominique Perrault
Architecture

type
station, public space, retails

construction
2013

77. Circumvesuviana Terminus Building

Corso Giuseppe Garibaldi 387
80142, Naples

open to the public

+39 081 200991
enteautonomovolturno@
legalmail.it
www.eavsrl.it

 1 / 2 > Garibaldi

 Circumvesuviana >
Napoli Porta Nolana

This building is the terminus of the Circumve-suviana Railway line that links the city centre with a large number of surrounding towns. The structure is set back from the street creating a small square on the very busy Corso Giuseppe Garibaldi. Its position was dictated by the intersection of the road and railway systems. The façade is aligned with the street and is dominated by a wide, con-tinuous, exposed concrete band that seems suspended above the glass entrance below, thanks to an elegant system of projecting beams supported by seven triangular ele-ments set inside the entrance and aligned in the direction of the railway lines. The clever structural façade design determines all the architectural elements of the building and provides a lightweight effect with strong visual impact. The complex is completed by a 14-storey, polygonal, glass and aluminium tower in strong contrast with the horizontal design of the main building that houses the actual station, ticket offices, café-bars, and access stairways to platform level, located one floor below.

© Giuliana Vespere

architects
Giulio De Luca,
Arrigo Marsiglia

type
station

construction
1975

78. The Fish Market

Piazza Duca degli Abruzzi
80142, Naples

external viewing only

 195 > Volta-Lucci

Designed by the master of Neapolitan Rationalist architecture, Luigi Cosenza, this building is a fine example of its avant-garde approach in line with the most modern international trends of its time.

The design is inspired by classical architecture with a rather austere style, and is renowned for the enormous vaulted roof over the vast central space. This space formed a covered market place originally destined for wholesale fish sales, although it also included 12 stores for retail sales, positioned on the side near the piazza. The entrances for the public and for transporting produce were placed on opposite sides of the centre space, on the lengthwise walls. The market was provided with light through the semi-circular glass brick gables of the vaulted roof and long slots in the roof spine. These slots were eliminated during roof replacement, and this aspect, plus other superfluous additions, have altered the original design considerably. Unfortunately, the building has been abandoned for some time and is waiting to be assigned a new purpose.

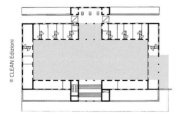

© CLEAN Edizioni

© Giuliana Vespere

architects
Luigi Cosenza

type
retail

construction
1935

79. Casa del Portuale

Calata Marinella
80133, Naples

external viewing only

This building is located in the eastern part of the city in a fragmented urban context, typical of city ports, and is dominated by the 17th century steeple of the Chiesa del Carmine. Originally constructed to house the port administration, archives and mecanographic centre, today it is in a state of neglect. It is one of the finest examples of contemporary Neapolitan architecture and the symbol of Aldo Loris Rossi's architectural development.

The complex building is composed of a central glazed prism in which other pure geometrical forms are inserted. These include semicircular disks and massive cylinders that cross the entire structure. The heavy concrete sections that contain structural and technical elements, projecting from the fragile central core, create a dynamic effect. This building is a visionary architectural work, that strongly recalls technological monumental Futurist design or utopic megastructures.

 151 > Marina-Mercato

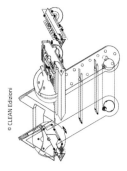

© CLEAN Edizioni

architects
Aldo Loris Rossi

type
offices

construction
1981

80. Brin69

Via Benedetto Brin 53 - 69
80142, Naples

partly open to the public

+39 081 203657
info@eccellenzecampane.it
www.eccellenzecampane.it

 2 > Gianturco

This project involves the recovery and conversion of a large decommissioned plant in the ex-industrial area of Naples on the eastern side of the city. The principle idea was to create a contemporary building that would provide a development incentive for the area under social-economic decline, acting as a driving model for possible regeneration projects.

The large building contains office, spaces and advanced services companies, innovative start-up businesses, and a food centre to showcase and sell regional gastronomical products of excellence. The vast internal space has been organised over several floors on various levels, catering to different requirements, and features a suspended internal garden, 5 metres high and 200 metres long, planted with a row of tall trees. Brin69 is a vibrant structure that has transformed a polluted industrial plant into sustainable architecture through vegetation, natural sunlight through large glass walls and roofing, water features and breezes that flow through the garden to the building.

© Archivio Vulcanica

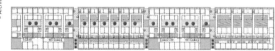

© Benato s.a.s

architects
Vulcanica architettura

type
retails, offices

construction
2016

81. San Giovanni Campus at the University of Naples Federico II

Corso Nicolangelo Protopisani 70
80146, Naples

open to the public

contactcenter@unina.it

 2 > San Giovanni

This intervention is part of a far greater urban redevelopment scheme in the east of Naples and involves the construction of a modern engineering faculty, which will include specialised laboratories, lecture halls, a multimedia auditorium, underground parking, and a planted and furnished public park. The industrial complex that previously occupied the area was not connected with the context, as the perimeter was mainly composed of blind walls. The new university campus, whose first lot was completed in 2016, wants to form a link between the urban fabric and the new green spaces within the site. The buildings, with continuous ventilated façades, located along the edges of the area to form the urban partition, are designed to maintain accessibility from the streets around the perimeter and to echo the traditional architecture of the city with its piazzas and inner courtyards.
Corbellini srl signed the technical plan, while Fabio Mastellone di Castelvetere curated the variations and additional projects that were necessary in order to comply with current regulations.

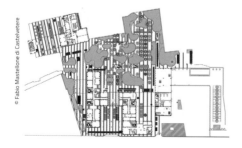

© Fabio Mastellone di Castelvetere

© Salvatore Giordano

architects
Ishimoto Europe, Ishimoto
architectural & engineering
firm, Francesco Scardaccione

type
university

construction
2016 / in progress

82. Ospedale del Mare

Via Enrico Russo
80147, Naples

open to the public

+39 081 18775059
dir.san.ospedaledelmare@
aslnapoli1centro.it
www.aslnapoli1centro.it

Circumvesuviana >
Vesuvio De Meis

The intervention curated by IAN+ for this innovative hospital focused on the entrance hall, the building dedicated to the distribution of internal pathways, a public square, and the hospital complex exterior. The project was based on Renzo Piano's design, commissioned by the Health Minister, Veronesi, in 2001. It planned for a hospital immersed in green surroundings, filled with light, and on a human scale, where the space would feel comfortable, not only for the patients, but also for families and medical staff.

The external space that acts as a filter between the hospital and the city, is a large square furnished with benches and metal shade pergolas, and paved with concrete and natural inert materials near the building, and green pebbles in resin closer to the street.

The façade of the new building is composed of blue and green glass panels in an irregular pattern. Inside the foyer, the radial layout on three levels is surrounded by the service and admittance areas, and acts as the departure point for access to the various hospital departments. Slender round steel columns are arranged around the circumference and large overhead skylights shed natural light into all levels of the iconic cylindrical glass structure.

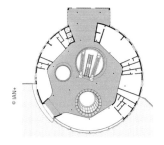

© IAN+

© Mario Ferrara

architects
IAN+

type
hospital

construction
2015

Museums

Museo Archeologico Nazionale – MANN
Archaeological museum
-
Piazza Museo 19, 80135 Naples

www.museoarcheologiconapoli.it
man-na@beniculturali.it
Tel +39 081 4422203

Museo Cappella Sansevero
Museum of 17th and 18th centurt art
-
Via Francesco De Sanctis 19-21,
80134 Naples

www.museosansevero.it
info@museosansevero.it
Tel +39 081 5518470

Museo Civico Gaetano Filangieri
Civic museum
-
Via Duomo 288, 80138 Naples

www.filangierimuseo.it
info@museofilangieri.it
Tel +39 081 203175

**Museo delle Arti Sanitarie
e Farmacia storica**
Medical history museum
-
Via Maria Lorenza Longo 5, 80138 Naples

www.museoartisanitarie.it
info@ilfarodippocrate.it
Tel +39 081 440647

Museo del Tesoro di San Gennaro
Ecclesiastical museum
-
Via Duomo 149, 80138 Naples

www.museosangennaro.it
info@museosangennaro.com
Tel +39 081 294980

Museo di San Lorenzo Maggiore
Museo dell'opera / archaeological excavations
-
Piazza San Gaetano 316, 80138 Naples

www.laneapolissotterrata.it
scavisanlorenzo@libero.it
Tel +39 081 2110860

Museo Duca di Martina
Museum of ceramics
-
Via Cimarosa 77, 80127 Naples

www.polomusealecampania.beniculturali.it
pm-cam.martina@beniculturali.it
Tel +39 081 5788418

Museo e Real Bosco di Capodimonte
Museum of ancient, modern
and contemporary art
-
Via Miano 2, 80131 Naples

www.museocapodimonte.beniculturali.it
mu-cap@beniculturali.it
Tel +39 081 7499111

Museo Madre
Museum of contemporary art
-
Via Luigi Settembrini 79,
80139 Naples

www.madrenapoli.it
info@madrenapoli.it
Tel +39 081 19737254

Certosa e Museo di San Martino
Museum of ancient and modern art
-
Largo San Martino 5, 80129 Naples

www.polomusealecampania.beniculturali.it
pm-cam.sanmartino@beniculturali.it
Tel +39 081 2294502

Theatres

Cinema teatro Augusteo
Piazzetta Duca d'Aosta, 80132 Naples

www.teatroaugusteo.it
teatroaugusteo@libero.it
Tel +39 081 414243

Teatro Bellini
Via Conte di Ruvo 14, 80135 Naples

www.teatrobellini.it
botteghino@teatrobellini.it
Tel +39 081 5491266

Teatro Diana
Via Luca Giordano 64, 80127 Naples

www.teatrodiana.it
segreteria@teatrodiana.it
Tel +39 081 5567527

Teatro Nuovo
Via Montecalvario 16, 80134 Naples

www.teatronuovonapoli.it
direzione@teatronuovonapoli.it
Tel +39 081 6581129

Teatro San Carlo
Via San Carlo 98/f, 80132 Naples

www.teatrosancarlo.it
biglietteria@teatrosancarlo.it
Tel +39 081 7972331

**Teatro Stabile (Mercadante /
San Ferdinando)**
Piazza Municipio, 80133 Naples / Piazza
Eduardo de Filippo 20, 80139 Naples

www.teatrostabilenapoli.it
info@teatrostabilenapoli.it
Tel +39 081 5510336

Restaurants

La Cantinella • • •
Via Cuma 42, 80132 Naples

www.lacantinella.it
info@lacantinella.it
Tel +39 081 7648684

• • • expensive
• • mid-range
• inexpensive

Mimì alla Ferrovia • • •
Via Alfonso D'Aragona 19/21, 80139 Naples

www.mimiallaferrovia.it
info@mimiallaferrovia.it
Tel +39 081 5538525

Palazzo Petrucci • • •
Via Posillipo 16/c, 80123 Naples

www.palazzopetrucci.it
info@palazzopetrucci.it
Tel +39 081 5757538

Al Poeta • •
Piazza Salvatore di Giacomo 135,
80123 Naples

www.ristorantealpoeta.com
enricovarriale@alice.it
Tel +39 081 5756936

Amici Miei • •
Via Monte di Dio 77/78, 80132 Naples

www.ristoranteamicimiei.com
info@ristoranteamicimiei.com
Tel +39 081 7646063

Hostaria La Vela • •
Calata Ponticello a Marechiaro 37,
80100 Naples

Tel +39 081 5751095

Il Ristorantino dell'Avvocato ··
Via Santa Lucia 115/117, 80132 Naples

www.ilristorantinodellavvocato.it
info@ilristorantinodellavvocato.it
Tel +39 081 0320047

Osteria della Mattonella ·
Via Giovanni Nicotera 13, 80132 Naples

Tel +39 081 416541

Trattoria da Nennella ·
Vico Lungo Teatro Nuovo 105,
80134 Naples

www.trattoriadanennella.it
trattorianennella@libero.it
Tel +39 081 414338

Hotels

Grand Hotel Vesuvio ···
Via Partenope 45, 80121 Naples

www.vesuvio.it
info@vesuvio.it
Tel +39 081 7640044

··· expensive
·· mid-range
· inexpensive

Hotel San Francesco al Monte ···
Corso Vittorio Emanuele 328,
80135 Naples

www.sanfrancescoalmonte.it
info@sanfrancescoalmonte.it
Tel +39 081 4239111

Palazzo Alabardieri ···
Via Alabardieri 38, 80121 Naples

www.palazzoalabardieri.it
info@palazzoalabardieri.it
Tel +39 081 415278

Costantinopoli 104 ··
Via Santa Maria di Costantinopoli 104,
80134 Naples

costantinopoli104.it
info@costantinopoli104.it
Tel +39 081 5571035

Renaissance Naples Hotel Mediterraneo ··
Via Ponte di Tappia 25, 80133 Naples

www.mediterraneonapoli.com
info@mediterraneonapoli.com
Tel +39 081 7970001

Santa Chiara Boutique Hotel ··
Via Benedetto Croce 23, 80134 Naples

www.santachiarahotel.com
info@santachiarahotel.com
Tel +39 081 5527077

Garibaldi 196 ·
Corso Giuseppe Garibaldi 196, 80142 Naples

garibaldi-196-apartment.hotel-naples.com
garibaldi196@gmail.com
Tel +39 389 1845126

Hotel MH design ·
Via Chiaia 245, 80121 Naples

www.mhhotel.it
info@mhhotel.it
Tel +39 081 19571576

Neapolitan Trips ·
Via dei Fiorentini 4, 80133 Naples

www.neapolitantrips.com
hotel@neapolitantrips.com
+39 081 19845933

Architectural offices

Alberto Izzo & Partners
Via Mergellina 2, 80122 Naples

www.albertoizzo-partners.it
info@albertoizzo-partners.it
Tel +39 081 7640609

Capobianco Architetti
Salita Santa Maria Apparente 35,
80132 Naples

capobiancoarchitetti@gmail.com
Tel +39 393 5673696

Corvino + Multari
Via Ponti Rossi 117a, 80131 Naples

www.corvinoemultari.com
info@corvinoemultari.com
Tel +39 081 7441678

Francesco Scardaccione
Via Francesco Girardi 29,
80134 Naples

www.scardaccionearchitect.com
info@scardaccionearchitect.com
Tel +39 081 4107654

Gambardella Architetti
Riviera di Chiaia 215, 80121 Naples

www.gambardellarchitetti.com
studio@gambardellarchitetti.com
Tel +39 081 415312

Gnosis progetti
Via Medina 40, 80133 Naples

www.gnosisarchitettura.it
gnosis@gnosis.it
Tel +39 081 5523312

**GSA Giancarlo Scognamiglio
Architettura**
Via Posillipo 66, 80123 Naples

www.gsarchitettura.com
winfo@gsarch.it
Tel +39 081 7690844

Od'A officina d'architettura
Via Paolo Emilio Imbriani 33,
80132 Naples

www.oda.na.it
info@oda.na.it
Tel +39 081 5512020

Paolo De Stefano
Via Antonio Beccadelli 23, 80125 Naples

paolo.destefano@gmail.com
Tel +39 081 5700861

Pica Ciamarra Associati
Via Posillipo 176 / Via Francesco
Petrarca 38, 80123 Naples

www.picaciamarra.it
f.damiani@pcaint.eu
Tel +39 081 5752223

Studio Associato Castagnaro
Via Maurizio de Vito Piscicelli 44,
80136 Naples

www.studiocastagnaro.com
segreteria@studiocastagnaro.com
Tel +39 081 5790866

Studio DAZ
Via Cisterna dell'Olio 25,
80134 Naples

www.studiodaz.it
info@studiodaz.it
Tel +39 081 5511447

Vulcanica architettura
Piazza Giacomo Matteotti 7,
80133 Naples

www.vulcanicaarchitettura.com
studio@vulcanicaarchitettura.it
Tel +39 081 5515146

Index by architect

Index by project

A. Siza, E. Souto de Moura, Studio DAZ
L. Cosenza / Od'A officina d'architettura

G. Scognamiglio
M. Capobianco, R. Dalisi, M. Pica Ciamarra
C. Cocchia, C. Blasi, M. Boudet, F. Cocchia, O. Frazzi,
M. Nunziata, G. Padovano, M. Pizzolorusso
Corvino + Multari
IAN+
A. Medrano, A. Canevari / E. B. De Felice, E. Amodio

F. De Simone
G. U. Arata
G. U. Arata
D. Fontana
Alberto Izzo & Partners
-
A. L. Rossi, A. Pignalosa, L. Rivieccio
F. Seguro
-
-
Gambardella Architetti
S. d'Ascia, MWH
G. Vaccaro, G. Franzi
M. De Renzi, R. Avolio De Martino, R. Contigiani /
Gnosis progetti, A. Castagnaro
F. Fuga
Gnosis progetti

Od'A officina d'architettura
Studio Purini/Thermes, A. Aymonino, G. Neri,
N. Surchat
M. Dezzi Bardeschi, Gnosis progetti, R. De Fusco,
A. Castagnaro
Atelier Mendini
Vari
F. Di Salvo
Atelier Mendini
Ishimoto Europe, Ishimoto architectural &
engineering firm, F. Scardaccione
C. Cocchia

S. d'Ascia

C. Bazzani
C. Guerra
G. De Luca, A. Marsiglia
L. Cosenza
L. Cosenza
G. Scognamiglio, A. Costa
O. Tusquets Blanca
F. Venezia

M. Capobianco / M. and L. Capobianco
Vari
D. Pacanowski
A. Avena
L. Cosenza, B. Rudofsky
P. Valente
A. Avena

Legend

- M Line 1
- M Line 6
- M MetroCampania NordEst Line Piscinola - Aversa
- M. Line 2
- Funicolars
- Circumvesuviana Railway
- Circumflegrea Railway
- Cumana Railway
- Regional and National Railway Network

- (✱) Art Station
- (⦿) Interchange nodes
- --- Escalators

- 🚌 Bus terminal
- ⛴ Boat service
- ✈ Airport shuttle Port - Central Station - Airport

Stations

Aversa Centro
Mugnano
Piscinola
Chiaiano
Frullone
Colli Amin
Policlinico
Rione Alte
Montedor
Medaglie
Salvator Rosa
Quattro Giornate
Vanvitelli
Cimarosa
MON

Formia

Licola Torre-gaveta

Quarto
Quarto Centro
Pisani
Pianura
La Trencia
Traiano
Soccavo
Piave

C.so V. Emanuele
Fuorigrotta
Palazzolo
CHIAIA
C.so V. Emanuele
Parco Margherita
Amedeo

Pozzuoli
Bagnoli
Cavalleggeri Aosta
Edenlandia Kennedy
Mostra
Agnano
Augusto
Lala
Mergellina

Pozzuoli
Gerolomini
Cappuccini
Dazio
Bagnoli
Campi Flegrei
Leopardi

Torre-gaveta

MERGELLINA

Manzoni
P.co Angelina
S. Gioacchino
S. Antonio
Mergellina

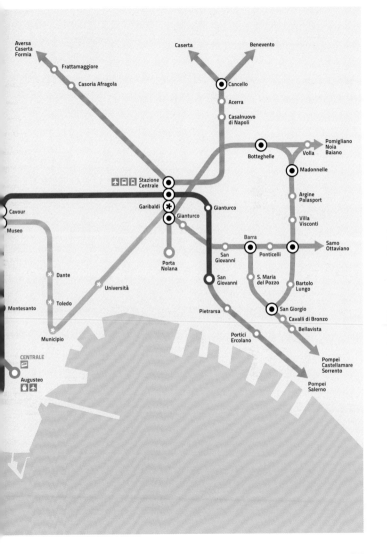

Aversa
Caserta
Formia

Frattamaggiore

Casoria Afragola

Caserta

Benevento

Cancello

Acerra

Casalnuovo
di Napoli

Pomigliano
Noia
Baiano

Botteghelle

Volla

Madonnelle

Stazione
Centrale

Garibaldi

Gianturco

Gianturco

Argine
Palasport

Villa
Visconti

Cavour

Barra

Samo
Ottaviano

Museo

San
Giovanni

Ponticelli

Porta
Nolana

Dante

San Giovanni

S. Maria
del Pozzo

Bartolo
Lungo

Università

Toledo

Montesanto

Pietrarsa

San Giorgio

Municipio

Cavalli di Bronzo

Bellavista

Portici
Ercolano

CENTRALE

Augusteo

Pompei
Castellamare
Sorrento

Pompei
Salerno

215

This volume was printed in February 2019
by CPZ Group, Costa di Mezzate (BG), Italy